Bradley Tyler Johnson

The foundation of Maryland and the origin of the Act concerning religion of April 21, 1649

Bradley Tyler Johnson

The foundation of Maryland and the origin of the Act concerning religion of April 21, 1649

ISBN/EAN: 9783337263713

Printed in Europe, USA, Canada, Australia, Japan

Cover: Foto ©ninafisch / pixelio.de

More available books at **www.hansebooks.com**

Fund-Publication, No. 18.

THE
FOUNDATION OF MARYLAND

AND THE

Origin of the Act Concerning Religion

OF

April 21, 1649.

Prepared for and partly read before the Maryland Historical Society

BY

BRADLEY T. JOHNSON,

A MEMBER OF THE SOCIETY.

Baltimore. 1883.

THE FOUNDATION OF MARYLAND.

Fund-Publication, No. 18.

THE
FOUNDATION OF MARYLAND

AND THE

Origin of the Act Concerning Religion

OF

April 21, 1649.

Prepared for and partly read before the Maryland Historical Society

BY

BRADLEY T. JOHNSON,

A MEMBER OF THE SOCIETY.

Baltimore, 1883.

PEABODY PUBLICATION FUND.

COMMITTEE ON PUBLICATION.

1882-83.

J. W. M. LEE,
HENRY STOCKBRIDGE,
BRADLEY T. JOHNSON.

PRINTED BY JOHN MURPHY & CO.,
PRINTERS TO THE MARYLAND HISTORICAL SOCIETY,
BALTIMORE, 1883.

PREFACE.

THE investigation, of which the following paper is the result, was commenced under the decided bias toward the opinion that Cecil Calvert had prosecuted his enterprise of colonization actuated solely by material motives, and that the Act concerning Religion was, in fact, only the echo of the liberal sentiments of the Separatist or Independent section of the Puritan sect in England.

The records have forced me to the conclusions herein set forth.

It is possible that newly discovered evidence, hereafter attained, may require some modification of them. I do not consider that probable, but, on the contrary, think it will strengthen them. Materials for fuller information exist and are within reach.

The State of Maryland has undertaken the publication of our Archives, which are voluminous, under the supervision of the Maryland Historical Society as a Record Commission. The papers in the British State Paper office are becoming accessible through the Calendar, now being edited and published by the British Record Commission, so that in a few years a great mass of historical material will be open to the student.

The Maryland Historical Society has a Calendar of Maryland Papers in the State Paper office at London, prepared by Mr. Stevens, and presented by Mr. Peabody.

It also has a Calendar of Maryland Archives prepared by the Rev. Ethan Allen under the direction of Dr. Alexander, containing a summary of the contents of six thousand manuscript pages of our Records.

But besides these sources of information, there is an immense mass of material, valuable and interesting, which has never been available to Maryland historians, or students of Maryland History.

The Archives of the Society of Jesus, and of the Sacred Congregation of the Propagation of the Faith at Rome, of the Province of the Society in England at Stonyhurst, of the Archbishopric of Canterbury, and of the Bishopric of London and of Zion College, contain invaluable information, as do the papers of the British Museum.

In the autumn of 1839, Dr. Alexander saw in one of the rooms of the British Museum, in one of the rooms on the ground floor, two considerable chests marked "CALVERT PAPERS." In 1861, when he instituted search for them and their contents, they had disappeared. The custodians of the Museum had, in the meantime, changed, and those then in charge supposed that they must have been sent there for sale, and being refused, were taken away. So we have lost trace of them.

But they must still exist, in private hands, or in some public collection.

An intelligent and energetic inquiry would recover them.

All these materials for our history ought to be collected and published.

The State might well charge itself with this duty. But it is not too much to hope that some Marylander of wealth and culture will come forward, and entitle himself to the thanks of this and future generations, by instituting measures by which all of the valuable material above indicated may be recovered, collected and given to the public.

Such an undertaking is worthy the ambition of those who, in this age, as patrons of culture and of art, succeed those merchant princes who led the Italian Republics in the renaissance of literature, science and thought.

The paper herewith submitted, prepared for and partly read before the Maryland Historical Society, has been prepared and revised under the constant pressure of professional engagements, and hence its many imperfections.

But it is an honest effort to contribute something toward the illustration of the early history of my native State, a history which the impartial observer accepts as an epoch in the development of civilization, and is the glorious heritage of every Marylander.

THE
Foundation of Maryland

AND THE ORIGIN OF THE

ACT CONCERNING RELIGION

OF

April 21, 1649.

THREE theories are advanced to account for the adoption of the principle of Religious Liberty in the Foundation of Maryland.

First. That Lord Baltimore, having acquired a principality, in order to develop it by speedy settlement, and promote his fortune, proclaimed and promised the largest liberality in grants of land and liberty of conscience to all who would emigrate to and colonize his new possessions.

"Lord Baltimore, as far as we can see, went into the task of colonization as a great English landed proprietor of the better sort administers his estates, conscientiously, and with a due regard to the welfare of the persons on his territory, but without any special sense of responsibility towards the community."[1]

"Yet there can be no doubt of the fact of religious toleration in Maryland at the very outset, and there were two very good reasons for its existence. The all powerful Lord Proprietary and the principal men in Maryland were Catholics, and Catholicism was oppressed and hated in England. To oppress Catholics would have been gross folly on the part of the Protestant colonists, and to oppress Protestants would have been ruin to the proprietary. Religious toleration in Maryland must be attributed solely to the very common-place law of self interest; and that this theory is the correct one, the subsequent history of the Colony amply proves."[2]

Second. The Puritan theory that the Protestants having the numerical preponderance in the Colony in 1649, proclaimed freedom of conscience as the fundamental law of the new commonwealth, being moved thereto by a profound conviction of its justice and the example of the Puritans in England.

---

[1] Doyle's English Colonies in America, London, 1882, p. 276.
[2] Lodge's History of the English Colonies in America, New York, 1882, p. 97.

"It was in 1649 that the Maryland Act of Toleration was passed, which, however, prescribed the punishment of death for any one who denied the Trinity. Of the small legislative body which passed it, two-thirds appear to have been Protestant, the recorded numbers being sixteen and eight respectively.

"The Colony was open to the immigration of Puritans and all Protestants, and any permanent and successful oppression by a handful of Roman Catholics was altogether impossible. But the Colonial Act seems to have been an echo of the order of the House of Commons at home, on the 27th of October, 1645, that the inhabitants of the Summer Islands, and such others as shall join themselves to them, 'shall, without any molestation or trouble, have and enjoy the liberty of their consciences in matters of God's worship; and of a British ordinance of 1647.'"[1]

Third. The Roman Catholic theory that Lord Baltimore, being a devout Catholic, actuated by a desire to provide a refuge for his oppressed co-religionists, founded a Catholic Colony, composed in the main of Roman Catholics, and by his own authority, with their co-operation and sympathy, and through the promptings and teach-

---

[1] Mr. Gladstone, in his "Preface to Rome and the Newest Fashions in Religion," p. 8.

ings of his Church, adopted and proclaimed the Law of Religious Liberty to all Christians of every creed and sect whatsoever, as the fundamental institution of the new State.

"Such was the Commonwealth founded by a Catholic, upon the broad moral law I have here laid down — that faith is an act of the will, and that to force men to profess what they do not believe is contrary to the law of God, and that to generate faith by force is morally impossible."[1]

An examination of the records of the Province of Maryland from 1635 to 1660; of those of the English Province of the Society of Jesus, which were partly given to the public in the "Records of the English Province," edited and published in London, in 1878, by Henry Foley, S. J.; of some original manuscripts in the Records of Stoneyhurst; of the historical papers printed in "The Woodstock Letters,"[2] and of the latest investigations of this subject by Bancroft, Lodge and Doyle, proves that each of these theories is erroneous, and that while each contains some ingredients of truth, neither one sets forth the real causes which developed the early institutions of

---

[1] Cardinal Manning in "The Vatican Decrees in their bearing on Civil Allegiance," p. 88.
Clark's "Gladstone and Maryland Toleration," p. 4.
[2] See Appendix A.

Maryland. The facts and circumstances surrounding and accompanying the foundation of Maryland, demonstrate, beyond reasonable doubt, that Cecil Calvert, second Lord Baltimore, determined to devote his fortune and his life to founding a State in America, over which he and his posterity should preside, based upon the institutions of English liberty, and where all the guarantees and safeguards by which it had been secured and protected, from before Magna Charta until his time, should be enjoyed, and where they should be forever preserved. His object was not only to secure a refuge for persecuted Roman Catholics, hounded from every hundred in the three kingdoms, where they might enjoy their religion in peace, but the larger and nobler one, that a great State should grow up, where the rights, franchises and liberties of Englishmen, freedom of person, security of property, and liberty of conscience, the right to *habeas corpus* and trial by jury, to be taxed only by themselves, and to be unmolested in their homes and their families, should be secured and guaranteed to all its people forever.

Under the ancient institutions of England, beginning in the Germanic fatherland, developed and strengthened by generations of freemen, fortified and defended by ages of armed assertion and forcible maintainance, every man's house was his castle, every man's person was sacred, every man's rights were his own. These institutions had been transplanted from the forests of Germania and the country of the English, to the Island in the North Sea, and had been deeply rooted and flourished there. They had always been protected by trial by jury. When attacked or temporarily overthrown, they had been guaranteed and fortified by *habeas corpus*, and when the power to make laws for all the people, belonging of right to the Germanic host, then descending to the folkmote, had been usurped by king or baron, the free spirit of a free people had secured and asserted them in a Parliament, which representing *them* and executing *their* will, had alone the right to lay taxes or grant aids or subsidies, or to appropriate any portion of the private property to the public use. For the great charter was the assertion of recovered rights, not the claim of new ones. In the thirty years just preceding the grant of the Charter of Maryland, all these institutions of England had been the subject of universal and bitter discussion. The Petition of Right, asserting them, passed in 1628, five years before the date of the charter.

The great mass of the people were denied the most elementary franchises of Englishmen. The rights of trial by jury and *habeas corpus* were becoming doubtful. Power to levy taxes without the vote of Parliament was being claimed. A majority of the people dissenting from the State Religion, part adhering to the old, part professing an advanced form of the new, were oppressed and harried, fined and imprisoned, and denied every right guaranteed by the Great Charter and re-asserted in the Petition of Right.

The oppressed always appeal to the rule of right as against the rule of power—the minority always plead the protection of constitutions—and Puritan and Roman Catholic, in England at that time, claimed, asserted or relied on those ancient institutions of liberty which their ancestors had brought with them to England, and had guarded so jealously ever since.

The right of conscience is but the logical consequence of the right of person or the right of property. If a man cannot be constrained of the liberty of his person or of the free use of his own property, it follows, by irresistible logic, that he must be allowed the liberty of his thoughts, which are intangible, and which cannot be affected or controlled by human law.

Therefore it was that idea of Religious Liberty grew up with both Puritan and Roman Catholic, as the absolutely necessary consequence of the enjoyment of these rights, franchises and liberties of Englishmen, which were their birthright. Thus it was that the principle of freedom of conscience, as a perfect concrete polity, grew up in the mind of Lord Baltimore. Sir Thomas More, in the Utopia, had distinctly foreshadowed it as the controlling influence in an ideal State. The facts prove that Cecil Calvert was deeply imbued with a love and veneration for the free institutions of England, and a conviction of the wisdom, justice and expediency of the guarantees which had protected them in all the struggles of the English people.

He knew from experience, as he understood by reason, that neither liberty nor its safeguards could be enjoyed while men were constrained in their religious convictions, and he adopted the principle of Religious Liberty, as covered by and included in the guarantees of the Great Charter, not that there could be liberty of conscience without security of person and property, but that there could be no security of person and property without liberty of conscience.

His devotion to the institutions of English liberty were consistent with his fidelity to the dogmas and the faith of the Roman Catholic Church. Just a century before, Sir Thomas More, Lord High Chancellor, had proved his loyalty to free institutions and to the Church alike.

Under his lead the Commons had protested against the legislation of the clergy in convocation, without the King's assent or that of his subjects, and reform in the Church was pressed by the Chancellor. He resisted the pretensions of the Church to extend the jurisdiction of the canon law by convocation, whereby laws were made by priests alone and not by the representatives of the people, and whereby causes, matrimonial and testamentary, were swept within the circle of ecclesiastical authority, and trial by jury was in many cases denied in questions of right. But while he urged reform in the relations of the Church to the State, "his love for freedom, his revolt against the growing autocracy of the Crown, the very height and grandeur of his own spiritual convictions, all bent him to withstand a system which would concentrate in the King all the power of Church and State, would leave him without check and would make him arbiter of the religious faith of his subjects. . . . . The later revolt of the Puritans against the King worship, which Cromwell established, proved the justice of the prevision which forced More, in the spring of 1532, to resign the post of Chancellor. . . . . By the Act of Supremacy of 1534, authority in all matters ecclesiastical was vested solely in the Crown. The supreme ecclesiastical jurisdiction passed to the Chancellor, who already exercised the supreme civil jurisdiction. . . . . More believed that the sacrifice of liberty and justice was too dear a price to pay for even religious reform. .... Triumphant in all else, the monarchy was to find its power stop short at the conscience of man. The great battle of spiritual freedom, the battle of Protestant against Mary, of the Catholic against Elizabeth, of the Puritans against Charles, of the Independents against Presbyterians, began the moment that More refused to bend, or deny his convictions at the King's bidding. He refused to take the oath that the marriage of Catherine was against Scripture and invalid from the beginning." [1]

So Sir Thomas More had been steadfast in his maintainance of all the liberties of Englishmen, while he had sealed with his blood his loyalty to his faith and had denied by his death the right or power of King or Parliament to compel the conscience of man.

Henry More, the great-grandson of the great Chancellor, was high in authority in the Society of Jesus during the most eventful years of Lord Baltimore's struggles, and what influence the martyrdom of his ancestor for freedom of conscience had on him, how the Chancellor's theories of government, as shown by his thinly veiled allegory of the Utopia, were accepted by him, we have no means of knowing. We do know

---

[1] 2 Green's History of the English People, 148-165.

that he was in constant communication with Lord Baltimore, and we have further proof that the latter's efforts, from the beginning, were to lay the foundation of the new Commonwealth securely and deeply upon the ancient institutions, not of feudal England, but of free England.

Instead then of the foundations of Maryland having been laid on a policy of colonization and material development, or as the consequence of religious movement in England, or as the result of the teachings and practices of the Roman Catholic Church, the light now shed upon the contemporaneous actors, their motives and their acts, enable us to see that Lord Baltimore, from the very initiation of his enterprize, deliberately, maturely, and wisely, upon consultation and advice, determined to devote his life and fortune to the work of founding a free English State, with its institutions deeply planted upon the ancient customs, rights and safeguards of free Englishmen, and which should be a sanctuary for all Christian people forever.

This purpose, wisely conceived, maturely considered and bravely persisted in, through all obstacles, explains everything that has heretofore appeared ambiguous in the career of Lord Baltimore.

It explains his sympathy at first with the royal cause in the civil war, and his speedy withdrawal from it, and his communications with the Parliamentary leaders, and it makes intelligible the apparent changes in his policy in his attitude towards his colony, when he first claimed the right to initiate laws and then abandoned it, and then reasserted it.

It gives us to understand why he persisted in his efforts to have the General Assembly adopt the codes which, on two several occasions, he prepared and sent out for its consideration, and it explains the reason why he changed the officers of his government, the commissions of his officers, their official oaths and the conditions of plantation, upon which lands could be acquired.

The struggle between the Catholic power of Spain and Queen Elizabeth had demonstrated the loyalty of the English Catholics, who were among the first to take arms and the most zealous in support of her throne. The result had been to kindle a flame of patriotic devotion to England in the hearts of all her people, and no portion of them were more devoted to her institutions than the Roman Catholic nobles and commons.

The struggle between Charles I. and the Parliament, from 1625 to 1629, had resulted in the abeyance of Parliamentary Institutions in England. The decision of the Court of Star Chamber in the case of John Hampden and the ship-money, in 1638, had settled the law that taxes could be levied without the consent of the people, and the lives, liberties and property of all Englishmen were at the disposal of an absolute king. Free institutions in France and Spain had before then succumbed to the power of the monarchy, and men generally believed that they had ceased to exist in England. The fury of religious bigotry persecuted Puritan and Roman Catholic alike, and the only hope and refuge of both was the ancient right of Englishmen prior to and under the Great Charter and the ancient institutions of their native land. Great multitudes prepared to transfer themselves to America. Lord Warwick acquired the Connecticut Valley. Lord Say and Sele and Lord Brook arranged to emigrate, and John Hampden bought a large tract of land on Narragansett Bay.

It seemed as if England was no longer a place where men could be free, and while the Protestants were thus preparing to seek new homes for themselves in the wilderness, the Roman Catholics, impelled by the same necessity and driven by even more cruel laws, began to concert among themselves measures by which a sanctuary for their religion and their liberties could be provided on the same continent where so many other Englishmen were finding refuge.

Among their leaders, lay and ecclesiastical, measures began to be concerted. James I. had, in 1623, granted to Sir George Calvert the charter of Avalon, for a settlement in Newfoundland. Avalon was the name of the ancient district in Somersetshire, where, according to the legend, St. Joseph of Arimathea had landed and first planted the Christian faith in Britain.

Calvert made voyages to Newfoundland, and attempted a settlement; with him were sent three Jesuit priests. But the rigor of the climate forced him to abandon his undertaking, and in the winter of 1629–30, with his whole colony, he sailed south in search of a more genial clime. On his arrival in Virginia, he was refused permission to remain, because he declined to take the oath of supremacy and abjuration. He left his wife there and returned to England, and then began again the effort of the English Roman Catholics to provide for themselves a place where they could enjoy peace and liberty.

In February, 1630, Baltimore, with Lord Arundel of Wardour, applied to the Attorney General for a grant of land south of the James river, within the boundaries of the Province of Carolana, "to be peopled and planted by them, with permission to erect Courts."[1]

Sir Thomas Arundel, first Baron Arundel of Wardour, was surnamed "The Valiant," having

---

[1] Sainsbury's Calendar of British State Papers.

been created by Rudolph III., Emperor of Germany, a Count of the Sacred Roman Empire, as a reward for having taken a Turkish standard, with his own hands, in a battle near Gran, in Hungary. His mother was daughter of the Marquess of Dorset. His wife was daughter of the Earl of Southhampton. His son married a daughter of Somerset, Earl of Worcester, and his daughter, Anne Arundel, married Cecil Calvert, son and heir to the first Baron of Baltimore.[1]

With them, assisting by counsel and all the power of the Society of Jesus, was Father Richard Blount, Provincial of the English Province. The ancient family of the Blounts is said to take its rise from the Blondi, or Biondi of Italy, and they from the Roman Flavii, both so called from their fair hair. They were Lords of Guisnes, in France, and came over with the Conqueror. One of the line was steward to Edward II., and in the family were the Baronies of Mountjoy and the Earldom of Devonshire. In the veins of Richard Blount ran the blood of Norfolk, of Howard, and of Warwick. He was a graduate of Oxford, a classmate of Laud, the Archbishop of Canterbury, who was a protegé of his family, and for forty years directed

---

[1] Burke's Peerage — Arundel of Wardour.

and controlled the movements of the Roman Catholics in England. He converted Thomas Sackville, Earl of Dorset and Lord High Treasurer under Elizabeth and James I., and received into the bosom of the Church, Anne, Queen Consort of James I. At his death, in 1638, his remains were laid to rest, by special permission of Queen Henrietta Maria, in her own chapel in Somerset House.[1] This great connection, bound together by blood or marriage, kinsmen and co-religionists, combined the greater part of the great historical houses of England whose roots and branches reaching down to the remotest times, spread and ramified throughout the Kingdom. They were the heads of the peerage, the controlling authority in the Church and the leaders of the Roman Catholics in England. Under their influence, directed and assisted by the great social and religious forces which they represented and controlled, this attempt was made to provide a country where Roman Catholic Englishmen might live and enjoy the liberty and institutions of their ancestors.

The visit of Baltimore to Virginia was undertaken for the purpose of exploration in carrying out this enterprise. With him, the Provincial sent Father Andrew White and two other Jesuit

---

[1] Troubles of Our Catholic Forefathers, first series, p. 188-202.

priests, to examine the location of the proposed Roman Catholic Refuge.¹ In company with Baltimore, Father White and his associates explored the country north of the James and on both sides of the great bay of the Chesapeake.

They reported to the Provincial that the land was pleasant to look upon and fitted for the homes of a happy people.²

Unfortunately, Arundel died, November 7, 1630, and the benefit of his co-operation and assistance was lost.³ But the influence represented by him survived. Baltimore, encouraged by Father Blount and the great families of the Roman Catholic Peerage, continued the undertaking in his name alone.

He obtained the grant of the country on the Chesapeake, and caused his charter to be prepared, in substance a copy of that of Avalon. Before it passed the Great Seal he died, and on June 20, 1632, it issued to his son, Cecil Calvert, the second Lord Baltimore.

The provisions of that charter are well known. It secured to the Proprietary the princely jurisdiction and rights of the Palatinate of Durham.

---

1 " Baltimore had three priests with him in Newfoundland, and emigrated, with his whole colony, to Virginia."—Doyle's English Colonies in America, p. 278-9.

2 Woodstock Letters, vol. 9, p. 158, Archbishop Carroll's narrative.

3 Appendix B.

It guaranteed to the freemen all the rights, franchises and privileges of natural born Englishmen, and the right to participate in the making of their own laws and the imposition of their own taxes. The Charters of Elizabeth, of James I. and of Charles I., secure to colonists under them the rights of natural born Englishmen. The charter of Avalon, copied into the Charter of Maryland, is the first which provides for the right of representative assemblies.[1]

Just before the Charter of Maryland was issued, the Petition of Right was passed, in 1628, reiterating the claims of the Great Charter, which had been reasserted in thirty-two statutes since the reign of Henry I. The minds and hearts of the great body of Englishmen, Protestant and Roman Catholic alike, were then intent on preserving these great muniments of liberty.

When the Charter was issued, Lord Baltimore must have been impressed with the imminent peril impending over all the free institutions of England.

Therefore it was that the undertaking of Arundel, and Baltimore, and Blount, of Norfolk,

---

[1] The charter of Elizabeth to Sir Walter Raleigh, of 1584; to the Virginia Company, of 1606, of 1609, of 1621; of New England, of 1620; of Massachusetts, of 1629; of Carolana, of 1629, all guaranty the Rights of Englishmen.— Charters and Constitution U. S., 1878.
Charter of Avalon, 1 Scharf.

and of Howard, committed to his hands alone, broadened and widened far beyond the aspirations of his father, or the hopes or expectations of his father's associates. Instead of founding a Roman Catholic colony in Maryland, as the Pilgrims had founded a Puritan colony in New England, it became apparent to his wise mind, that to secure any liberty at all, he must secure it by the safeguards, which experience had proved, had protected it for so many centuries in England, and that to make these safeguards more efficient than they had been in England, there must be extended to all, the rights of all men to the rights of person, of property and of thought. He therefore determined to invite all men, of all Christian people, to emigrate to the new colony, under the conditions of the Charter.

That Charter was considered in itself to be a license to liberal opinions. It was understood to carry with it, especially to Roman Catholics, the right to enjoy their religion without let or hindrance. And its liberal provisions were made the ground of grave objections, to permitting them to enjoy the benefits of it.

He laid the subject before the Provincial for advice and assistance, and after consideration of the objections advanced, that officer determined that it was expedient to give the whole power of the Society of Jesus to assist the enterprise, as modified by Baltimore. We have the record of the objections urged to the Charter, and to permitting Roman Catholics to emigrate under it, and to settle in the new Province, with the answers which were made to those objections, and as the document has never been published before, it is considered best to insert it here at length. Between June, 1632, and the fall of the following year, the following paper was prepared by the Provincial, for the guidance of the Society and Lord Baltimore:

Objections Answered Touching Maryland.

Object. I. It may be objected that the Lawes against the Roman Catholikes, were made in order to their Conformity to the Protestant Religion, for the good of their Soules, and by that meanes to free this Kingdome of Popery, rather than of their persons, but such a Licence for them to depart this Kingdome, and to go into Maryland, or any Countrey where they may have free liberty of their Religion, would take away all hopes of their Conformity to the Church of England.

Answer. It is evident that reason of State (for the Safety of the King and Kingdome) more than of Religion, was the cause and end of those Lawes, for there are no such against divers other professions of Religion in England, although they be as different from the doctrine of the Protestant Church, established by Law in this Kingdome, as that of the Roman Catholiques is: And the Reason of State appears also in the Nature of most of those Lawes, for they expresse great doubts and jealousies of the said Roman Catholiques affection to, and dependence on a forraigne power, and tend therefore most of them, to disinable them (by confining, disarming, etc.) from plotting or doing any mischiefe to the King or State, and to Secure their allegiance to the King by oathes etc., and the penalties of divers of them, are abjuration of the Realme, which puts them out of the way of Conformity to the Church of England. Moreover Conversion in matter of Religion, if it bee forced, should give little satisfaction to a wise state, of the conversion of such convertites, for those who for worldly respects will breake their faith with God, doubtlesse will do it, upon a fit occasion much sooner with men, and for voluntary conversions, such Lawes could be of no use, wherefore certainely the safety of King and Kingdome, was the sole ayme and end of them.

Object. II. Such a licence will seem to be a kind of tolerations of (at least a conivance at) Popery which some may find a scruple of Conscience, to allow of in any part of the Kings Dominions, because they esteeme it a kind of idolatry, and may therefore conceive that it would scandalize their Bretheren and the common people here.

Answer. Such scrupulous persons may as well have a scruple to let the Roman Catholikes live here, although it be under Persecution, as to give way to such a licence, because such banishment from a pleasant, plentiful and ones owne native Countrey, into a Wilderness among savages and wild beasts, although it proceed, in a manner from ones own election, yet, in this case, when it is provoked by other wayes of persecution, is but an exchange rather than a freedom of punishment, and perhaps in some mens opinions, from one persecution to a worse. For divers Malefactors in this Kingdome, have chosen rather to be hanged, than to goe into Virginia, when upon that condition they have bin offered their lives, even at the place of Execution, and they may with more ground have a scruple of Conscience to let any of the said Roman Catholiques to go from hence unto France, which few or none certainely can have in contemplation of Religion only, and this Parliament hath given passes to divers of them for that purpose, that being more properly the Kings Dominions than is all that great part of North America, wherein Maryland is included, unto which the crown of England lays claim, upon the Title of discovery only, except such part thereof as is actually seated and possessed by some of his subjects, and therefore in the Preamble of the Lord Baltimores Patent of Maryland, the enlargement of the Kings Dominions is recited as a motive of the grant, which inferres that it could not so properly be esteemed his dominions before, as when by virtue of such a grant it should be planted by some of his subjects, and if it be all the Kings Dominions notwithstanding; then why have not such scrupulous persons a scruple to suffer the Indians (who are undoubted idolators) as they do, to live there, which if they cannot conveniently prevent, as without question they cannot, unless it be by granting such a licence, they may as well suffer those whom they may esteeme Idolators, as those whom they and all other Christians whatsoever repute and know to be so, to inhabit and possesse that Countrey. Moreover they may also (as well as in this) have a scruple to treat or make, or continue a League, or to trade with any Forraigners of that Religion, because in their opinions they are Idolators, or to permit the Public Ministers of any such Forraigne Prince or State to have the free exercise of their Religion while they are in England, and may cease giving scandall to others by such tolerations or conivances: All which nevertheless we see done, even in these times, and allowed of, as well by the Parliament as the King, upon reason of State, for the good and safety of this Realme.

So may this Licence be also thought by such persons a good expedient for the same purpose. And if any (of the weaker sort) should be scandalized at it, the scandall would be, *acceptum* not *datum*, and therefore not to be regarded by a wise and judicious Prince of State.

Object. III. By it the Kings revenue will be impaired in losing the benefit which the said Lawes give him, out of Recusants Estates, while they continue in England of that possession of Religion.

Answer. The end of those Lawes was not the Kings profit, but (as is said before) the freeing of this Kingdome of Recusants which deprives the King of any benefit of them, so as his Majesty will have no wrong don him by such a Licence, because he will lose nothing by it, of what was intended him by the said Lawes: this is no ancient Revenue of the Crowne, for it had inception but in Queen Elizabeths time, and conformity or alienation to a Protestant deprives the King of this Revenue. If there were no crimes at all committed in England, the King would loose in any fines and confiscations, whereby his Revenue would also be impaired (wch in the other as in this branch of it is but casuall) and yet without question, the King and State would both desire it. The same reason holds in this, considering what opinion is had here of the Recusants, wherefore it cannot, with good manners be doubted that his Majestie will in this business preferre his owne benifitte, before that which the State shall conceive to be convenient for his safety, and the publique good.

Object. IV. It would much prejudice this Kingdome by drawing considerable number of people, and transporting of a great deale of wealth from hence.

Answer. The number of the Recusants in England is not so great, as that the departure of them all from hence would make any sensible diminution of people in it, and the possession in Religion would make them lesse missed here. If the number were great, then consequently (according to the maximes of this State) they were the more dangerous, and there would be the more reason, by this means to lessen it: And if it bee but small (as indeed it is) then their absence from hence would little prejudice the Kingdome in the decrease of people, nor will such a Licence occasion the transportation of much wealth out of England, for they shall not need to carey any considerable summes of money with them, nor is it desired that they should have leave to do so, but only useful things for a Plantation, as provisions for clothing and Building and Planting tooles etc. which will advantage this

Kingdome by increase of trade and vent of its Native Commodities, and transferre the rest of their Estates by Bills of Exchange, into Bankes beyond Sea, which tends also to the advantage of the Trade of England, for more stock by this means will be employed in it.

Object. V. It may prove dangerous to Virginia and New England, where many English Protestants are planted, Maryland being situated between them both, because it may be suspected that the said Roman Catholiques will bring in the Spaniards or some other forraigne enemy to suppresse the Protestants in those parts, or perhaps grow strong enough to doe it of themselves, or that in time (having the Government of that Province of Maryland in their hands) they may and will shake off any dependance on the Crown of England.

Answer. The English Colonies in New England are at least 500 miles, and that of Virginia 100 miles distant from Maryland, and it will be a long time before planters can be of leisure to think of any such designe, and there is little cause to doubt, that any people as long as they may live peaceabley under their owne Government, without Oppression either in Spiritualls or Temporalls, will desire to bring in any Forraigners to domineire over them, which misery they would undoubtedly fall into, if any considerable forraigne Prince or State (who are only in this case to be feared) had the possession of the English Collonies in Virginia or New England; But the number of English Protestants already in Virginia and New England, together with the poverty of those parts, makes it very improbable that any Forraigne Prince or State, will bee tempted to undergo the charge and hazard of such a remote designe, it being well known that the Spanish Collonies in the West Indies are farther distant than Europe is from thence: if any danger were to be suspected in that way from the said Recusants, the like suspition of bringing in a Forraigne Enemy into England may (as indeed it hath often beene) be had of them; while they are here, for the difference of scituation may balance the difference of the power, between this Kingdome, and those parts, for the accomplishing of such a designe, and certainely (of the two) it were much better to throw that hazard, if it were any, upon Virginia and New England, than to have it continuee here, much lesse cause is there to feare that they should grow strong enough of themselves to suppresse the Protestants in those parts: For there are already at least three times as many Protestants there, as there are Roman Catholiques in England. And the Protestants in Virginia and New England are like to increase much faster by new supplies of people yearley from England, etc. than are the Roman Catholiques in Maryland, Moreover although they should (which God forbid and which the English Protestants in those parts will in all probability be still able to prevent) shake off any dependance on the Crowne of England; yet first England would by this means be freed of so many suspected persons now in it.

Secondly, it would loose little by it: And lastly even in that case, it were notwithstanding more for the Honour of the English Nation, that Englishmen, although Roman Catholiques, and although not dependant on the Crowne of England, should possesse that Countrey than Forraigners, who otherwise are like to do it: for the Swedes and Dutch have two severall Plantations already in New England, and upon the confines of Maryland, (betweene the English Colonies in New England and Maryland) and doe incroach every day more and more upon that Continent, where there is much more Land than all the Kings Protestant Subjects in all his Dominions (were they there) would be able to possesse. But the assurance of Protection from the Crowne and State of England, upon all just occasions, either of danger from a Forraigne Enemy, or of any wrongs which may be done unto them by his Majesties Protestant Subjects in those parts, and the benefit of trade with England for yearly supplies, without which they will not be able to subsist, will be strong tyes, if there were no other, to bind them to Continue their dependance on it.

Moreover the mouth of the Bay of Chesapeake being but narrow, and at which all ships that come to Maryland must enter, is within the precincts, and power of the Colony of Virginia.

And the Planters of Virginia will by the accesse of so many neighbours be much advantaged, because their Cattle and many other commodities which they abound in and have no vent for, and which this New Colony will stand in need of will, by this meanes yeeld them good rates, which now are of little value to them, wherefore certainely they will fear no prejudice but will be glad of such a market for improvement of their estates, though perhaps some petty Merchants here, traders to Virginia, may conceive it prejudicial to them, and therefore may make religion, and other vain pretences of danger to Virginia, or this State, the cloake of their avarice, to hinder this design: whereas in truth it can be nothing else, but feare of the increase of the commodities they deale in; and consequently of an abatement of the prices that may incline them to oppose it.[1]

This paper proves that the Charter of Maryland was then considered and treated, as securing liberty of conscience to Roman Catholics. It proves further, that the Society of Jesus undertook to further and extend the planting of the colony, with full knowledge that the principle of religious toleration was to be adopted as one of the fundamental institutions of the Province, and toleration for Roman Catholics carried with it, of necessity, toleration for all Christians.

The Provincial of Jesuits therefore agreed to assist in adopting and applying this principle in Maryland.

---

[1] Stoneyhurst MSS. Anglia, vol. iv.

Baltimore, statesman, lawgiver and thinker far in advance of his time, alone saw, knew, and understood, that liberty of conscience was impracticable without liberty of person, and security of property, just as the existence of the latter would, beyond doubt, develop and protect the former.

Therefore it was that he organized his first expedition, in accordance with these views, composed exclusively of disciples of neither faith, but with the influences and material power of both fully represented. The first colony was numerically Protestant; politically, socially, and religiously it was Roman Catholic. The physical power was Protestant, the intellectual and moral and political control was Roman Catholic.

The expedition consisted of his brother, Leonard Calvert, as Governor, Jerome Hawley and Captain Thomas Cornwaleys, as Assistants, with twenty gentlemen of good fashion, and probably two hundred others, mechanics, laboring men and indentured servants. The gentlemen were Roman Catholics. Among them were Fathers Andrew White, John Altham and Thomas Copley, priests of the Society of Jesus.

Of the two hundred others, the majority of them were Protestants.

After the ships with the colonists had sailed, the London "Searcher," Edward Watkins, caused them to be brought back, and administered the oaths of allegiance, supremacy and abjuration, to one hundred and twenty-eight, all who were on board. After his departure, the ships stopped at the Isle of Wight, and took on board the remainder of the colonists. Those who took the oaths were certainly Protestants. No Roman Catholic could have taken them. So one hundred and twenty-eight, out of two hundred and twenty were Protestants. The memorial of the Provincial, Father Henry More, to Rome, written in 1642, with full knowledge of all the facts, expressly states "that the affair was surrounded with many and great difficulties, *for in leading the Colony to Maryland, by far the greater part were heretics.*"[1]

And in a paper prepared by Father Andrew White, in Maryland, in 1641, transmitting "TWENTY CASES" to the Provincial of England for advice, he says: "*And whereas three parts of the people in four at least are heretics.*"[2]

There can be no doubt, therefore, that Baltimore organized his first expedition with a majority of Protestants.[3] Under the Charter, only the freemen were allowed political rights, and the Catholics had the majority of freemen.

---

[1] Records of the English Province S. J., vol. 3, series 7, p. 361. Stoneyhurst MSS. Anglia, vol. iv, n. 108 K.

[2] Records of the English Province S. J., vol. 3, series 7, p. 362. Stoneyhurst MSS., vol. iv., n. 108 b.

[3] Appendix C.

Of the officers of government, Calvert, of course, was a Roman Catholic.

Neill states that Jerome Hawley was a Protestant, and that his brother, William Hawley, signed the Protestant declaration in 1650, but I find no proof of it. He stayed only a short time in the colony, was Treasurer of Virginia in 1638, died in August, 1638, and Captain Thomas Cornwaleys was his administrator in Maryland.[1]

The other assistant, Captain Thomas Cornwaleys, was a Protestant. He is the most interesting figure in early Maryland history. From the first settlement he filled a conspicuous place in our annals, until 1659, when he returned to England. He was the leader in the Assembly, the commander of the expeditions against Claiborne and the Indians, Councillor, Lieutenant-General and Assistant Governor, *ad interim*. In the first Assembly, he insisted upon the rights of the Assembly to introduce, consider, and determine upon such measures as they deemed proper, and denied the right of the Proprietary to originate laws. He claimed that the colonists were entitled to all the rights, franchises and liberties of native born Englishmen, and under his lead the Common Law of England was adopted as

---

[1] See Appendix to Streeter Papers, p. 119.

the rule of judicature of the Province. This included Magna Charta and the Petition of Right. Under his lead again, the Code sent out by Secretary Lewgar, in 1637, was rejected in 1637-38, while the material provisions of it were reported by a committee, of which he was chairman, and were adopted.[1] He may therefore be considered as the most influential character in the first expedition, not excepting the Governor.[2] Among the gentlemen, were representatives of the ancient and honorable Catholic houses of Gerard, of Wintour, of Wiseman and of Darrell. The policy which was to guide and control the new Commonwealth, was thus fully illustrated in the very act of its foundation.

II.

The first settlement was made at St. Maries, in March, 1634[o. s.], and a General Assembly of the "Freemen" was held there in the winter or spring of 1635. Of it no record remains. There is a statement in a subsequent statute that it adopted the Common Law, as the rule of right, and security in the colony, and a copy of an Act to attaint William Claiborne, passed by

---

[1] Streeter Papers. The proceedings of the Assembly of 1637-8, printed in full.

[2] Appendix D.

the General Assembly of 1637, has been discovered in England, which refers to the existence of the Assembly of 1635. I doubt whether it was called under warrant of the Proprietary.

The Colony was not yet ready for a legislature, and it would seem the better opinion, that he deferred calling an Assembly until he had matured, in consultation with Richard Blount and those other advisers and coadjutors in his undertaking, such measures as were necessary to carry out the broad and wise policy which he had determined upon, and to which he henceforward devoted himself. His assistants and counsellors were learned in the law and history of England, and lovers of her free institutions, as is proved by the propositions which were adopted as proper to be the foundation of the institutions of Maryland.

The papers, from this time forward, which emanated from Lord Baltimore, were the production of a lawyer, a statesman, and a wise lawgiver, versed in the lore of English records, and informed in the development of English institutions. They exhibit an intelligent plan and a settled policy in Lord Baltimore.

In August, 1636, he issued Conditions of Plantation, setting forth the terms upon which lands could be acquired, and providing that grants of one, two or three thousand acres to any adventurer should be erected into a manor, with all the rights, franchises and privileges appurtenant to an English manor, and among them the right and duty to hold a Court Baron and a Court Leet. Forms of the grants for a manor and the Court Baron and Court Leet were such in the then conditions of plantation as "presidents" for Governor Calvert to follow.[1]

He had, in some proclamation or public declaration, before then, published as inducements for colonists, that they would be granted liberal donations of lands, and be secured in the enjoyment of their religion, for the first clause of these conditions refers to his former promises, and declares that by this latter document he provides for fulfilling them. Under this power, numerous manors were created, with Courts Baron and Courts Leet. One was held on the Isle of Kent, and we have the record of the Court Leet of St. Clement's Manor.[2]

Having thus provided for securing the freemen in their estates and homes, he devoted himself to the preparation of a Code of Laws for their adoption, which should secure them their rights and properties above the encroachment of any power, lay or ecclesiastical.

---

[1] Lib. A, B, and H, fol. 61.
[2] In the Md. Hist. Society Records.

The body of laws prepared for him are the work of a hand and head well acquainted with the technical knowledge of the Common Law, and learned in the origin, the cause and the inestimable value of English institutions. These laws comprise the subjects, of securing the liberties of the people, of providing for General Assemblies of all the freemen, for the settlement of the Christian Church, for titles to and descent of lands, for the succession of the goods of intestates, and for the dividing of the Province into political subdivisions to be called baronies, and for the ratification and preservation of the manors, manor rights and manor courts, created under the Charter, and which were intended to provide proper police regulations for communities and separate settlements in the wilderness.

This Code, so well considered, was committed to the hands of John Lewger, who arrived at St. Maries on the 28th of November, 1637. Lewger was born in London in 1602, and was a Bachelor of Arts of Trinity College, Oxford. He became a Bachelor of the Faculty in 1632, and then received the gift of a handsome benefice in Essex.

William Chillingworth, one of the fellows of Oxford, was Lewger's intimate friend, and when he became reconciled to the Church of Rome, Lewger followed him, about 1634. When Chillingworth subsequently returned to the Church of England, Lewger remained a Roman Catholic, and in April, 1637, he was commissioned by Lord Baltimore, Secretary of the Province, Register of Grants of Land, Collector of the Customs and Receiver of Rents, and, with Jerome Hawley and Thomas Cornwaleys, a member of the Council.[1]

Upon his arrival, all the freemen of the Province were summoned by name to a General Assembly to meet at St. Maries. And here it is well to remark upon the location of political power among the colonists at that time.

I have shown that of the two hundred and twenty adventurers, who sailed in the autumn of 1634, one hundred and twenty-eight of them were Protestants. But very many of the Protestants were servants, owing service and labor to their masters, some by indenture of apprenticeship and some by contracts of service in consideration of transportation to the new country. None of them were summoned to the General Assembly, for none were summoned but "freemen," and in the proceedings of some of the subsequent Assemblies, the claim was expressly made by a servant of the right to participate in it, and it was held that none but "freemen" were entitled to membership.

---

[1] Streeter Papers, p. 224.

The Journal of the Assembly records the names of ninety freemen present or represented by proxy. Inasmuch as all the freemen "were summoned to appear by virtue of writs to them directed," and those who failed to do so were amerced and appeared by proxy, it is reasonably certain that of the two hundred and twenty or more colonists, only ninety were freemen, and it is equally certain that a large majority of the freemen were Roman Catholics.

The three Jesuit priests, Fathers Andrew White, John Altham and Thomas Copley, "gentlemen," were summoned and "appeared by Robert Clarke, gent, and excused their absence by reason of sickness.[1]

The Assembly met on the 25th of January, 1637 [o. s.], that is the January following Lewger's arrival.[2] The laws brought out by the Secretary were submitted to them. They were rejected as a whole, and a committee appointed "to prepare a draught of some laws to be sent up to the Lord Proprietor." Whereupon the House adjourned on January 29th to February 8th, and then to March 12th, when the committee reported forty-two statutes, which were

---

[1] Streeter Papers. The full proceedings of this Assembly printed from the records.

[2] The legal year began in England on March 25, until 1751, when an Act of Parliament passed that it should commence on the 1st of January.

passed, but never assented to by his Lordship. From the titles of the statutes, for the body of them has not been preserved, it is clear that a committee could not have prepared them in the time taken by it, and that they were the same laws propounded through Secretary Lewger for their adoption. The Assembly thus asserted its right to initiate legislation, and at the same time agreed to the Code prepared, as we have seen, in England, with a deliberate and enlightened purpose.

The titles are, as shown by the record:

1. A Bill for dividing of the Province.
2. A Bill for the Bounding of Manors.
3. A Bill for Assigning of Manors.
4. A Bill for the Order to be Observed in the Assignments.
5. A Bill for the Peopling of Manors.
6. A Bill for the Supporting of Manors.
7. A Bill for Settling of the Glebe.
8. A Bill Against Aliening of Manors.
9. A Bill for Baronies.
10. A Bill for Assigning of Freeholds.
11. A Bill for the Demesnes of the Lord Proprietary.
12. A Bill for Building of the Town.
13. A Bill for the Erecting of the Fort.
14. A Bill for Planting of Corn.
15. A Bill for Restraint of Liquors.

16. A Bill for Military Discipline.
17. A Bill for Ordering the Payment of Tobacco.
18. A Bill for Services to be Performed for Manors and Freeholds.
19. A Bill for Assurance of Titles to Lands.
20. A Bill for the Liberties of the People.
21. A Bill for Swearing Allegiance to our Sovereign.
22. A Bill for Descending of Land.
23. A Bill for Succession to the Goods of Intestates.
24. A Bill for Public Ports.
25. A Bill Touching General Assemblies.
26. A Bill for the Probate of Wills.
27. A Bill for Civil Causes.
28. A Bill for Payment of Debts contracted out of the Province.
29. A Bill for Punishment of ill Servants.
30. A Bill for the Attainder of William Claiborne.
31. A Bill for the Limiting of the Times of Service.
32. A Bill for Confirming the Sentence against Thomas Smith.
33. A Bill for Corn Measures.
34. A Bill for Fees.
35. A Bill for Payment of forfeitures.
36. A Bill for Treason.

37. A Bill for Capital Offences.

38. A Bill Allowing Clergy for some Capital Offences.

39. A Bill for Arbitrary Punishment of Enormous Offences.

40. A Bill for Punishment of Certain Crimes, in the County Court.

41. A Bill for Punishment of Lesser Crimes.

42. A Bill for Support of the Lord Proprietary.[1]

Most prominent among these statutes are those relating to Baronies and to Manors.

Lord Baltimore has been criticised for thus attempting to transplant decaying feudal institutions to the virgin soil of the new continent. But his critics have been alike ignorant of the institutions they condemn and of the scope of his intent. Bozman has proved that the "Bill for Baronies" was, most probably, a proposition for the creation of political subdivisions, such as were then and are now known in Ireland as Baronies, where Baltimore held estates, and where he was engaged in the enterprise of colonization. The manor was not a feudal institution at all. It is the evolution of the Germanic Mark. The territory held by the community was called the Mark, and was the common property of all the

---

[1] Bacon's Laws, 1637.

freemen. They lived together in the village in the centre of their lands, and each was entitled to a share for the purpose of cultivation, but all had the right to the enjoyment of the woods, the pastures and the meadows. Hence the right of common. Every such Mark became a political unit, and every freeman had his place in the Assembly of the Mark, which regulated all the internal business of the partnership and of the relations that arise from it. It was called the Mark Moot. From the Mark descended the township. It was the form in which the older institution was transplanted to England.

Its headman was the *tun-gerefa* (our sheriff), who was chosen by the freemen at first, but afterwards by the lord. The business of the township was transacted by the townsmen, assembled in "*gemots*," which made "*bye-laws*" for the police regulations of the whole and elected the *gerefa* (sheriff) and "*bydel*" (beadle) to enforce them.

After the conquest, the name of the existing organization was changed to manor, and its English "gerefa" to the Norman "steward," its ancient "bydel" to "bailiff." Their offices and names were retained by subordinate officers, the "reeve" and the "bedell."

"No new England was created; new forms displace but do not destroy the old, and old rights remain, although changed in title and forced into symmetry, with a new and pseudo-historical theory. The townsmen retain their customary rights of common in pasture, wood and meadows, and their participation, in a less degree, in the government and police of the manor."

The Court Baron and the Court Leet replaced the Mark Moot and the township "gemot." In the Court Baron, "by-laws" were made and other local business transacted; in the Court Leet was exercised the criminal jurisdiction, and it was not until the reign of Henry II. that the Justices of the King or the national authority were permitted to exercise jurisdiction over manor tenants, and manor rights and police. They were attended by jurors, and "the principles of legal procedure applied in them contained the whole accumulation of ancient custom as well as Norman novelty."[1]

The township meeting of New England, and the County Court of Virginia, and the English South, are to-day the direct descendants of the Mark Moot, the Gemot, the Court Baron and the Court Leet.

At the County Court all the people assemble once a month. The public business is trans-

---

[1] Stubbs' Const. Hist., 33, 85, 89, 91, 399.

acted by the County Court, police regulations enforced, jurors drawn, roads supervised, accounts of public officers — the sheriff, the coroner, the road-supervisor and the constable examined, and their conduct criticised or corrected. The people transact their private affairs — settle old contracts, make new ones, hear speeches from any one who chooses to speak on any imaginable topic, and "receive the accounts of their stewardship" from their servants in Congress or the State Legislature. Settlements run from court day to court day, and contracts are made to be performed on court days.

No broader, deeper, more influential institution for a free people exists anywhere to-day. By it all the freemen are brought into frequent contact, for the purpose of the exchange and diffusion of ideas and information, and by such frequent communication, they are enabled the more readily to protect their rights, by combining to redress wrongs, correct abuses and institute necessary changes and reforms.

Thus the institution of manors and manor rights had arisen at the very birth of the race, long before a branch of it emigrated to England, and had for centuries been the Watch and Ward of Common Right. Baltimore proved his sagacity in seeking to plant them in Maryland, as well suited to an infant colony in a savage wilderness. They were, in fact, the customs of a warlike emigration settling itself among enemies in a strange land.

Thus had the English brought them to England, and so Baltimore sought to have the English carry them to Maryland.

While the Proprietor had the undoubted right to create manors and manor courts by grant, he evidently desired to have these institutions, so well adapted to the necessities of the colonists, accepted by the freemen themselves, and thus rest upon the broad and secure basis of popular ratification.

We see that the first Code prepared by Lord Baltimore of which we have record provided for securing the liberties of the people, for a General Assembly of all the freemen, in person or by their delegates, to make laws for the general concern, and for creating manors with the appropriate courts, to make and administer community police regulations.

The first Code of Virginia was a compilation from the martial law in force in the Low Countries, brought in by Lord Delaware, having been prepared by the Virginia Company for the government of the Colony in 1610, and which was confirmed with additions by Sir Thomas Dale.

In the hands of an unscrupulous Governor, says Doyle, it would have given rise to a sys-

tem of tyranny little more merciful than that
which goaded the Netherlands into revolt. The
whole Code was evidently a system designed for
the restraint of a brutal and wasteful soldiery,
made up in a large measure of adventurers,
without country or fixed allegiance.[1]

Vague complaints, says he, were made at a
later day of the numbers who perished under
the "Egyptian slavery and Scythian cruelty"
of these laws. It is probable, however, that
they only applied to the company's servants,
and not to the independent planters, who had
settled at their own expense, or to the indented
servants on their estates. They were, nevertheless, the fundamental institutions of the new
State, provided by the governing power for the
foundations of its society.

The first form of government, both of Ply-
mouth, and of Massachusetts Bay, was a theoc-
racy, with a union of Church and State, based
upon the principles and rules of the Mosaic
law. From the beginning, the foundations of
Maryland were laid upon the free representative
institutions of England, and the English people,
by the wise forecaste of the Proprietary.

Why the laws passed by this Assembly did
not receive his assent, we do not know. They

---

[1] Doyle's English Colonies in America, pp. 139-140.

were enacted in March, 1637 º·ˢ·, 1638 ᴺ·ˢ·. He must have received notice of the refusal of the freemen in General Assembly to permit him to originate laws during that spring or summer, and on August 21. 1638, he wrote to Leonard Calvert, authorizing him to assent to all laws passed by the freemen in his name, which laws "should remain in force until he should disassent thereto, under the great seal of the province." [1]

This warrant reached the province in the fall of 1638, and a new General Assembly was at once called, which met February 25, 1638 º·ˢ·, 1639 ᴺ·ˢ·.

In this "gemot" or "folk-mote" of all the people of Maryland, was vested all the legislative power of the State. The Proprietary had abandoned his claim under the Charter, of confining their consideration, discussion and action to such subjects, as *he* chose to submit to them, and had admitted their claim to consider, discuss and propose any subject *they* thought fit, and to propose such matters to him as *they* determined to be necessary.

The very first act of this first people's Legislature, of this first popular government in Maryland, the very first act of any legislative power

---

[1] Assembly proceedings, 1637 to 1658, p. 86.

here, was the passage of an act for establishing that power on the sure and solid right of all the freemen, to participate in the making of the laws by which they were to be governed.

It is the same act touching General Assemblies sent out by Lewger the year before, and rejected by the Assembly which met January 25, 1637-8, as has been stated, but which was afterward reported by the committee and passed by the House, but never assented to by the Proprietary.

It is entitled "An act for establishing the House of Assembly, and the laws to be made therein."

It provides that "the Burgesses to be elected by the freemen, who consent to the election, and the gentlemen summoned by his Lordship's special writ, shall be called the House of Assembly. And all acts assented to and approved by said House, and *afterward* assented to by the Lieutenant General in the name of his Lordship, shall be adjudged and established for law, to have the same effect as if his Lordship *and all the freemen of this province* were personally present and did assent thereto."

Such act was to be considered *first* the act of all the freemen, and *afterward* of his Lordship.

This act was passed the very first day the Assembly met—February 25, 1638-9.

The Code rejected by the last Assembly was then considered. Those provisions relating to manors were omitted, and the most important provisions of it were enacted into our statute on March 19, twenty-one days afterwards. That ordinance stands as the first Code of Maryland law.

Bozman has remarked on it, but it has never attracted the attention, nor received the veneration which is due to it as the provision made by Cecil Calvert, for the foundation of the institutions of Maryland. More than the act concerning religion, it is the Magna Charta, the Petition of Right, and the Bill of Rights, all in one statute, and liberty of conscience in 1649, followed as the irresistible logical consequence of this great ordinance of 1638-9.

Section 1 declares that "Holy Church within this province shall have all her rights and liberties."

Section 2 required that all inhabitants should take the oath of allegiance to the King. It omitted the oath of supremacy which declared a belief in his Headship of the Church, and the oath of abjuration, which denied allegiance of any kind, to any other prince or potentate, civil or ecclesiastical.

Section 3 declares that "the Lord Proprietary shall have all his rights and prerogatives."

Section 4. "That the inhabitants shall have all their rights and liberties according to the Great Charter of England."

Section 5 secures to them the right to the common law.

Section 6 guarantees the right of trial by jury.

Section 7 asserts the civil jurisdiction over matters testamentary, and gives the Secretary power to prove wills, and grant letters of administration, over the estates of decedents, and section 14 provides for the manner of summoning and electing members of the General Assembly.

The declaration of the first section, "that Holy Church within this Province shall have all her rights and liberties," is but a reiteration of the first clause of the Great Charters of John, of Henry III., and of Edward I., which declares "that the Church of England shall have all her rights and liberties inviolate." It had been reiterated and reasserted by more than thirty Parliaments, and the wise statesman who directed the destinies of the infant State, put it on record among the first acts of its people, and Proprietary. "That the Church of England should be free," says Lord Coke, "means that all ecclesiastical persons within the realm, their possessions and goods, shall be free from all unjust exaction and oppression, but, notwithstanding, should yield all lawful duties to the King or any of his subjects."

It meant in Maryland, that the Christian Church should be free from unlawful interference by any temporal power whatever. It was a reiteration of the mandate of her Charter, that " nothing should be done contrary to God's Holy Religion," and, with that mandate, was the guaranty of liberty of conscience, to all Christian people in Maryland.

It is manifest that Lord Baltimore would never, in 1637 or 1638, have dreamed of establishing the Roman Catholic Church by law, in an English province, when the celebration of the Mass was a capital felony in England. The contemporaneous construction of the Charter by the Provincial of the Jesuits, the *personnel* of the first colonists, and of the first government all prove this.

I may say that sturdy Thomas Cornwaleys, who insisted on the right to the common law, and the statutes, who challenged the right of the Governor to prorogue the Assembly, who protested against the introduction of the law of privilege of Parliament, would never for a moment have consented to the establishment of that Church by law over him, and his Protestant family and servants.

It is equally clear that the Proprietary, the Governor, Mr. Secretary Lewger, the convert from the Church of England, nor the Catholic gentlemen, who composed the majority of the Assembly would not have consented to participate in establishing the Anglican Church over them.

The Proprietary, in his original proclamation inviting adventurers, had promised freedom of religion to all Christian men.[1]

In another proclamation, since the first settlement, he had prohibited "all unseasonable disputations in point of religion tending to the disturbance of the public peace and quiet of the colony, and to the opening of faction in religion."

In the preceding July, William Lewis, a Roman Catholic, had been fined 500 lbs. of tobacco for interfering, by opprobrious reproaches, with two Protestants, Francis Gray, a freeman, and Robert Sedgrave, a servant, for reading a Book of Protestant Sermons.[2]

The fundamental Constitution of the Colony therefore rested on liberty of conscience, as the consequence of liberty of person, and security of property, and the explicit invitation, engage-

---

[1] See Appendix A on Woodstock Letters.
[2] Proceedings 1637-1644—printed in full in the Streeter Papers, p. 212.

ment and official acts of the Proprietary; and Bozman is in error when he concludes that it was the intention by that statute to establish the Roman Catholic Hierarchy in Maryland.[1]

While the main provisions of the Code of 1637 were enacted in these two statutes of 1638, the Assembly failed to pass one of the most important of them.

The twenty-seventh of the bills proposed by Baltimore was "A bill concerning the calling of General Assemblies."

Baltimore had seen the King dissolve Parliament in 1629. No Parliament had met in England since that year. A grave dread filled the hearts of all Englishmen, that no Parliament ever would meet again. He therefore sent out this bill, intended to become a perpetual law, by which Assemblies were to be called "once in three years at the least, and the freemen assembled therein to have the like power, privileges, authority and jurisdiction, in causes and matters arising within this Province *as the House of Commons have had, used, or enjoyed, or of right ought to have, use, or enjoy, in any matters which have at any time happened or risen within the realm of England.*"[2]

---

[1] 2 Bozman, 109.
[2] Bacon's Laws, 1638.

The definite and mature purpose of the Proprietary, to found a commonwealth, and transplant to it, all the rights and liberties of Englishmen, together with all the safeguards and guarantees of Parliamentary institutions, inherited and enjoyed by them, is no where more plainly and distinctly demonstrated than by this proposed law.

The Assembly in Maryland did not appreciate the necessity for it as fully as did the Proprietary in England, and they failed to pass it, but the very first act of the Parliament called in the succeeding year by the King, was to pass the "Act for Triennial Parliaments."

In the interval between the settlement at St. Maries, in March, 1634, and the meeting and adjournment of this General Assembly, various events had transpired which produced momentous results. The colony had been reinforced by numerous additions. The Jesuits, zealous in propagating their faith, and in proselytizing, had made many converts among the lower order of Protestants, and had been eminently successful among the Indians. Emperors and kings, with their people, had embraced the Cross, and been baptized into the Church.

As a natural consequence, great grants of valuable land were made by the aboriginal chiefs to the Fathers, who had converted them to the faith. King Pathuen had given them the valuable estate of Mattapany, in St. Mary's county, near the mouth of the Patuxent, where the Jesuits had stationed a mission, and besides that Thomas Copley, whose status as a Jesuit priest is not disclosed by the records, had demanded large grants under the conditions of Plantation of 1636, in consideration of transporting Andrew White, John Altham and others, thirty in all, in 1633, and Mr. John Knoles and others, to the number of nineteen, in 1637.[1] He had received grants of land for bringing into the Province fifty persons.

Under the conditions of Plantation of 1636 he received title to twenty thousand acres, and he held it to the use of the Society of Jesus. In January of 1637, when the Proprietary was preparing his Code of Laws, he commissioned John Lewger " Commissioner in causes testamentary, to prove wills and to grant letters of administration, &c."

The priests White, Altham and Copley, had been summoned by writ to the General Assembly of 1637–8, and had been excused on account of ill health, as we have seen.

By the Great Ordinance of 1638–9 it was enacted that the laws should be equally en-

---

[1] Kilty's Landholder's Assistant, p. 68.

forced against and concerning all persons, lay and ecclesiastical, without distinction, exemption or privilege to any.

Its twelfth section ratified the commission to Lewger, by providing "that the Secretary shall prove wills, and grant administrations, and use and appoint all power and means necessary or conducing thereto."[1]

The jurisdiction of the temporal authority, therefore, had been distinctly asserted by his Lordship's act over all ecclesiastical persons and their property, and over all causes testamentary, and over the administration of the estates of decedents. This had been done deliberately, in carrying out a mature policy.

This assertion of jurisdiction by the temporal Prince, over ecclesiastical persons and things on the one side, and the acquisition of lands from the Indians, and by Copley, for the use of the Jesuits on the other, made a distinct issue in Maryland that had been contested in England for six hundred years, and had only shortly before then been finally settled. It was the old question as to whether the Canon Law prevailed and was in force *jure divino* in a State, or whether it was only allowed so far as adopted by the Prince or State itself. Under all the circum-

---

[1] Lib. C. and W. H., fol. 65.

stances, it was, perhaps, natural that such a question should arise.

In the organized State of England it had been definitely settled, but in such a country as Maryland, then a savage wilderness, with a few hundred Christians, founding a new society upon Christian principles, which were to pervade, control, and direct it for all time, the enthusiasts who had braved the hardships of emigration, and the terrors of the unknown, by land and by water, to carry the Cross to the heathen, may well have believed that the power of the Keys, should prevail over the power of the Sword, and that their duty to religion and truth, required them to assert the supremacy of the ecclesiastical authority over the temporal power. At any rate, the missionary priests at once claimed that the Canon Law prevailed in Maryland *proprio vigore*, without the license, assent or adoption of Prince or people. It existed because it was the law of the Church. This was the old claim of the extension of the *corpus juris canonici* over England.

The body of the Civil and Canon Law is composed of selections from the Roman Institutes, together with the Decrees of Councils and the Bulls of the Sovereign Pontiff, issued from time to time. It asserts on behalf of the Church, by divine right, the exclusive jurisdiction over all ecclesiastical persons, things, and property. It protects or punishes priests as to common rights or common wrongs, while it equally punishes or protects laymen concerning ecclesiastical matters. Its jurisdiction over the persons of all priests, exempts them from amenability to the temporal courts. Its authority over all ecclesiastical matters, draws within its power, all laymen having concern in such matters.

Taking exclusive cognizance of all causes testamentary, the clergy, under this law, paid legacies to the Church or to pious uses before they paid creditors, heirs or legatees, and, assuming sole control of administration of the estates of decedents, the ordinary never rendered any account whatever of such estate, and it was absorbed to the uses of the clergy.

All questions of fact and law were tried under this system of law by judges who were themselves ecclesiastics, and trial by jury was as foreign to the spirit of the Civil and Canon Law, as it was unknown in ecclesiastical courts. This Code had never been assented to in England. The English never did agree to obey any laws, save those to which they had assented by King, Barons or Commons. Trial by jury and the right to be represented in the making of laws, were the fundamental institutions of the race.

Therefore, before the Norman conquest, the pretensions of Churchmen to extend the Canon Law to England, and the English, had never been assented to, and had universally been rejected.

From that epoch, there had been a constant struggle against the assertion of its jurisdiction. The Norman lawyer-ecclesiastics, the clerks, persisted in their effort to introduce it, but the conquered race resisted, as only institutions backed by manly men can resist, the effort to deprive them of their birthright — trial by jury and the right to participate in law making, and generation after generation, still struggled on against any law being enforced in England without the consent of King and Parliament.

Cognizance of causes testamentary was first given to the Ecclesiastical Courts by Henry I., and Stephen first agreed that the Roman Civil and Canon Law alone should govern them. Benefit of clergy, and exemption from lay jurisdiction of their persons, and property, became complete. But the Constitutions of Clarendon, A. D. 1164, greatly narrowed the clerical exemption, and Edward I. limited the jurisdiction of these courts, and compelled the ordinary to whom administration of intestate estates were committed, to discharge the debts due by the intestate in his lifetime.

But it was not until Henry VIII.'s time that the supremacy of the crown over the spiritual men and causes, and the abolition of all clerical exemptions was established.

Sir Thomas More led the Commons in their protest against the right of the Clergy in Convocation to legislate without the King's assent, or that of his subjects. And at last, Sir Edward Coke, in King's Bench, in Caudrey's case,[1] settled the law of England that "all causes testamentary and matrimonial are to be determined and decided by ecclesiastical judges according to the King's Ecclesiastical Law of this Realm."

This was the law of England. The question was whether it was, or could be in force in Maryland.

By the "BULLA IN CŒNA DOMINI," the Pope asserts full supremacy over all persons, and powers, temporal and ecclesiastical. That decree forbids all persons whatsoever, directly or indirectly, to violate, depress or restrain the ecclesiastical liberties or rights of the Apostolic See and Church of Rome, howsoever or whensoever obtained, or to be obtained, under pain of excommunication, and all who presume to oppose any of its provisions are left under the displeasure of Almighty God.[2]

---

[1] 3 Coke, 1.
[2] Streeter's Maryland Two Hundred Years Ago, p. 32.

The Jesuit Fathers, in this conflict of law, as they supposed, very naturally held on to the law which bound them, until it was shown that they were bound by the laws of England in this behalf. Great issues were at stake, and the discussion of them naturally aroused feeling. Secretary Lewger had been a Protestant. He was an Englishman—an educated scholar of the University of Oxford. He knew the history of the struggle in England against the authority of the Canon Law, against the exemption of ecclesiastics, their persons and their property from the temporal jurisdiction, the enormous abuses that had grown out of their usurpation of the exclusive cognizance of causes testamentary and matrimonial, and the great evils, political and social, produced by the holding of great estates in mortmain. He understood the policy of the Proprietary, which he had been selected and sent out to carry out—to transplant to Maryland all the safeguards against these abuses and the remedies for these evils, and the guarantees for liberty, which the experience of Englishmen had demonstrated to be necessary, to preserve their institutions, and which their sagacity had devised, their wisdom adopted, and their courage secured.

Therefore it was that Lewger, carrying out the purposes of the Proprietary, set himself against this claim of the authority of the Canon Law, and procured the Assembly to unite with Baltimore in asserting the supremacy of the temporal power of freemen, and Proprietary, in General Assembly.

He followed this up in the Assembly which met the following autumn on the 25th of October, 1640, by procuring to be passed the act touching marriage. The persons who can celebrate it, the parties who are permitted to marry, and the conditions upon which they may marry, are all declared and specified.[1] The whole subject of marriage thus passed under the control of the temporal authority.

He further insisted that all grants of land to the Jesuits should be vacated, whether to them from the Indians or from the Proprietary to Thomas Copley, who held the land for the use of the Society.

Baltimore pressed his policy that the Common Law of England should be the law for every body in Maryland, lay and ecclesiastical, and no great estates should grow up in mortmain, to be a future menace to the liberties and free institutions of the province.

Immediately after the adjournment of the General Assembly, Lord Baltimore brought the matter

---

[1] Lib. C. and W. II., fol. 69.

before the highest authority of the Church, and "petitioned the Sacred Congregation of the Propagation of the Faith in the name of the Catholics of Maryland to grant a Prefect and secular priests authority, to take charge of the Maryland mission." In August, 1641, permission was given Baltimore to remove the Jesuits, and the authority to take charge of Maryland issued to Dom Rossetti, Archbishop of Tarsus.[1]

In November, 1641, he issued Conditions of Plantation, to take effect in the following January, and they put in actual operation in Maryland all the provisions and prohibitions of all the Statutes of Mortmain, which had been enacted in England before that time.

The first four sections of these Conditions were duly published, and are recorded in their proper place in our records.[2] The fifth and sixth sections were never recorded, and we do not know how far they were published. They were fortified with an oath, of which no record exists. It would seem as if the provisions of mortmain, and the oath, were kept back on account of some fulminations of the *Bulla in Cœna Domini*, or in order to procure explanations from the authorities at home, both from the

---

[1] Records of the English Province S. J., Seventh Series, p. 366.
[2] Council Proceedings, 1636-1657, fol. 81.

Provincial of Jesuits, and from the Proprietary. The Conditions and oath are published here in full.

CONDITIONS proposed by the most Illustrious Lord Cecilius, Baron of Baltimore, Lord and Proprietary of the Province of Maryland in the parts of America to all and singular, who shall offer themselves for the new plantation in the aforesaid Province. These conditions shall begin from the feast of the Annunciation of the Blessed Virgin Mary, 1642, and shall continue in force until new or other conditions of plantation for the same Province shall be published under the hand and seal of the same Illustrious Lord.

1. In the first place any person descending of British or Irish parents, who at his own expense shall have passed, himself or his deputy, into the Province of Maryland with a number of able men between the ages of 16 and 50 years, of the same nation aforesaid respectively, who shall have been furnished and provided with arms and ammunition according to the schedule hereafter inserted: or with a number of women between the ages of 14 and 40: to every such person, whether man or woman, for each and every twenty persons whom he shall bring within the space of one year, shall be assigned a portion of good land, which shall contain two thousand acres English measure: which lands shall be erected into manors and shall be transferred to him or to her and to the heirs of both by a Grant under the seal of the said Province in perpetuum in Soccage, with all such Royalties and Privileges, as are usually belonging to manors in England: rendering and paying annually to his Lordship and his heirs a rent of forty shillings of good and legal money of England, which are to be paid in the commodities of the country, and of such

services as from common consent shall be shown to work for the public good.

2. Moreover every person descending of the aforesaid descent, who shall bring at his own expense, himself or herself, and a less number of persons, whether males or females, than the number of twenty, of descent aforesaid, of the same age, furnished and provided as above, he or she and the heirs and assigns of both in perpetuum for and in respect of themselves and of each of the persons aforesaid, shall receive fifty acres of land within the said Province, to be held under some manor of his Lordship within the said Province in free Soccage, by rendering annually and paying a certain rent of twelve pennies of good and legal money of England per year to his Lordship, and his heirs for each fifty acres in the commodities of the country, as above.

3. Moreover whoever of the descent aforesaid shall at his own expense bring children of descent as aforesaid, that is, boys below the age of sixteen years and girls below the age of fourteen years, shall receive for himself and his heirs for and in respect of each one of his children, so to be brought as above, twenty-five acres of land within the same Province, to be held from and under some manor of his Lordship within the said Province as above, under the annual rent of six pennies of good and legal money of England for each twenty-five acres, to be paid as above.

4. Moreover every person who shall claim for himself any portion of lands within the said Province of Maryland by virtue of the aforesaid conditions, shall obtain a Grant of the said lands so due to him or them as above, under the seal of the aforesaid Province within the space of one year after those lands have been thus due to them, and assigned and published in some part of the said Province, by the Lieutenant General of his Lordship, in defect of which in virtue of these conditions they lose the right to such lands forever.

This is as far as the record goes, except the list of arms, &c. The two omitted sections and the oath are as follows:

5. Moreover that no corporation, Society, Fraternity, Municipality, Political body (whether it be Ecclesiastical or temporal) shall be capable of or shall have the benefit, in virtue of the preceding conditions of plantation, of receiving for itself, of inheriting, of possessing or enjoying any lands in the said Province either in right of their own or of any other person or persons, for their own use, interest or benefit or in trust for them without farther particular and special license first had and obtained for this end under the hand and seal of his Lordship. And if perchance any such grant should happen to be given to or obtained by any Corporation, Society, Fraternity, Municipality, Political body (whether this be Ecclesiastical or temporal) or any person or persons whatsoever for their use, interest or benefit or in trust for them without such farther particular and special license, as above, first had and obtained, that then all such Grants of whatsoever land within the said Province so made, or to be made, as above, shall be by the very fact void to all intent and purpose.

6. Moreover that no person or persons whatsoever, whatsoever be their condition or state, nor their heirs nor assigns, shall give, concede, alienate any lands or tenements within the said Province, assigned or conceded or to be assigned or to be conceded to him or them to any Corporation, Society, Congregation, Fraternity, Municipality or body Politic (whether this be Ecclesiastical or temporal) or to any person or persons whatsoever in trust or to such use or uses or to any use or uses contained, mentioned or prohibited in any Statute of Mortmain made before in the Kingdom of England without particular and special license before had and obtained for this end under the hand and seal of his Lordship.

A Schedule of the Arms and Ammunition, which are intended and required by the aforesaid conditions to be provided and brought into the said Province of Maryland by all and each of the men between the ages of sixteen and fifty years, who shall be carried thither.

In the first place, one gun or Bastard Musket with a snaphance lock.

Moreover, ten pounds of gun-powder.

Moreover, forty pounds of leaden bullets, Pistoll and Goose shot, each sort some.

Moreover, one sword and belt.

Moreover, one Bandelier and Flask.

Given at London, 10th of November, 1641.

The Oath directed by instructions to be administered to all and each of those who are to hold the lands conceded to them and to be received from them before the granting of their Patents.

I, A. B., acknowledge the Most Illustrious Lord Cecilius, Baron of Baltimore, to be the true and absolute Lord and Proprietary of the Province and region of Maryland and of the Islands thereunto appertaining according to the chart and patents of his Lordship under the great seal of England, and I swear that I will not directly nor indirectly by myself or by any other person or persons, procure, accept, receive, obtain, possess or enjoy any lands within the said Province by force of any Grant whatsoever from any Indian or any other person not legitimately deriving a title from, through and under a Grant of his Lordship, or his heirs, the Lords and Proprietaries of this Province, and if I shall know or understand that any other person acts contrary to this, without delay I shall take care to make this known to his Lordship or to his heirs or to their Lieutenant Generals or to other Governors of the said Province for the time being. And as much as shall be in my power I will defend and protect the title, right and royal jurisdiction of his Lordship to and over the said Province and the Islands thereunto appertaining, according to the chart of his Lordship above mentioned. So help me God, &c., &c.[1]

The receipt of this document in the Province brought on a conference between the Governor, Leonard Calvert, Secretary Lewger and the Jesuit Fathers. The memorandum of that conference is preserved at Stoneyhurst, and is as follows:

EXTRACTS FROM THE DIARY OF MR. LEWGER AND FROM THE LETTERS OF THE BARON OF BALTIMORE.

The Governor and I visited those Religious men, in order to treat of some difficulties with them.

1. One of these was about the publication of the new Conditions of this Plantation or Colony. This publication was to be made by the Governor with regard to that article especially by which all concessions made thus far were made subject to the Law of *Mortmain*. The Governor solved this difficulty by adding this interpretation of the said article: namely, that the concessions already made or to be made according to former conditions were not included in it: but the article was only intended for this, that no one should be allowed to profit by these new conditions unless he would submit all his property (fundos), as well granted already as to be hereafter granted, to this condition of non-alienation. As this did not seem to be any new ordi-

---

[1] Stoneyhurst MSS. Anglia, No. 108a, Vol. 4.

nance or edict, but a mere proposition left to each one's choice, these Religious men did not think it was forbidden in the Bull *Cœna*, nor that those who promulgated it incurred any sentence of excommunication.

2. The second difficulty was as follows. Although the preceding was not subject to excommunication, a mortal sin could however be committed by those who would be the instruments of such promulgation, negotiation and procuration of the said proposition and contract, because certain obligations against piety and good morals would be induced by it, and therefore there might be a mortal sin on both sides: namely, on the part of him who would propose such a contract as well as on the part of him who would accept it. Those Religious men resolved this difficulty in this wise, that at present it seemed that there would be a mortal sin, but they would examine it more maturely, before they would give a definitive decision.

3. However it seemed to them that the oath, to be taken under all those instructions, which were to be made for the possession of property, could not at all be taken with a safe conscience, but that the sentence of excommunication pronounced in the Bull *Cœna* was incurred by those who would promulgate, exhibit, enter upon record, or in any way give their labor and help in promoting the same.

4. And now a new question arises about the fifth article of the new Conditions of this Plantation or Colony: namely, that no Ecclesiastical Society should be admitted to these Conditions or be capable of them, which article seems to mean some ordinance and caution. If this be found to be the case, then I think an obstacle must be put to the promulgation and execution of the said Conditions, and no one would dare to help them to obtain their existence and life, lest he should incur the excommunication of the Bull *Cœna*.[1]

---

[1] Stoneyhurst MSS. Anglia, Vol. iv.

At this discussion, Secretary Lewger propounded to the Fathers the propositions of Canon Law, which he declared were prepared at the instance of and propounded by order of Lord Baltimore.

These questions are as follows:

CERTAIN QUESTIONS propounded by Mr. Lewger, Secretary of the Illustrious Lord Baron, mention of which is made in the notes No. 7.

1. Whether a Catholic Layman can administer the office of or can serve as a magistrate in any region, where the Church cannot concede and preserve all its laws, and its due immunities?

2. Whether the exemptions of the clergy, as to their persons, lands, goods, domestics, the privilege of sanctuary or asylum both in a church and in their houses, are due to them immediately by divine law from Our Lord Christ; so that the instant princes become Christians, they are bound in conscience to approve and confirm, or at least to permit and tolerate this sort of exemptions: Or whether they enjoy these by the spontaneous gift or devotion of pious princes and States, so that immediately any region be made Christian, it is necessary that a grant be made by the prince of such exemptions and immunities, before the Ecclesiastics can claim them as due in conscience: And whether before such grant of the Prince, or approbation of such privileges, the temporal authority can practically oppose them, without sacrilege, or incurring the censures of the Bull Cœnæ Domini?

3. Whether the erection of tribunals, with external compulsory jurisdiction be part of the power of the Keys left by Our Lord Christ to His Church; or whether it be part of the Sword placed by God in the hands of Princes, and by them granted to those in spiritual orders; and if an ecclesiastical tribunal should be

erected in such region with such power of external compulsory jurisdiction, whether the Prince could erect it of his own authority or rather should it be done by special commission of a delegation of the Papal Chair?

4. Whether in such a region, those Catholics who are parts of the general convention or Parliament, can give their consent to establishing laws about testamentary cases, and especially to a law declaring that what was left of the goods of the deceased, after all debts were paid and legacies fulfilled, should be given to the public use of the temporal state, and not to pious purposes as is done in Catholic countries?

5. Whether those Catholics who are part of the Parliament in such region, can consent to a law prohibiting any one from levying, or in any manner paying a lay or temporal tax to Ecclesiastics or Religious Houses, without the license of the Prince, by annulling all gifts and conveyances made in any other manner.

6. Whether Catholics who are members of the general assembly or Parliament, in such region, can consent to laws upon matrimonial causes, as those requiring the publication of the banns for political reasons, and prohibiting marriage without such publication of the banns, or license obtained from a Lay Commissioner, or limiting the degrees of consanguinity within which marriage should not be contracted, or determining cases of espousals, divorce, and the like?

7. Whether Catholics who are a part of the Parliament in such region, can consent to a law which for political reasons, prohibits a woman from capacity to be heir to lands, or declares they shall not hold them, unless she marry within a stated period, only leaving to them the power of selling and alienating these lands for their own greater emolument; and whether such a law be against conscience?

8. Whether in such region, a secular judge who is a Catholic, can examine and punish clergy, for any offence against the peace and dignity of the Lord Proprietary, or for a capital crime so far as the loss of life or limb, without incurring the censures of the Bullæ Cœnæ?

9. Whether Catholics, who are a part of the Parliament, in such region can consent to laws imposing general taxes for public revenue, for sustaining the Prince, or defending the Province, and whether ecclesiastical persons, and church lands, and goods, should be thought to be comprehended in such laws, because they are not in the law itself excepted; and whether a secular Catholic judge can grant letters, by which such taxes are imposed upon the lands or goods of ecclesiastical persons, or Religious Houses, without a special and express License from the Apostolic Chair?[1]

This discussion evidently took place after the Conditions of Plantation, November 10th, 1641, were issued, and it was forthwith transferred to England and thence to Rome. Immediately after the interview above described, Father White, the chief of the Maryland Mission, wrote a full account of all that had transpired in the Province since Lewger's arrival, and that was then transpiring, containing an account of the negotiations between the Governor, the Secretary, and Father White himself.

He embodied the points in a paper containing twenty cases of law, upon which he requested the advice of the Provincial of England, Henry More. The communication of Father White is as follows:

"The Cases."

In a country (as this is) newly planted, and depending wholly upon England for its subsistence, where there is not (nor cannot

---

[1] Stoneyhurst MSS. Anglia, Vol. iv.

be until England be reunited to the Church), any ecclesiastical discipline established, (by law of the Province or grant of the Prynce), nor Provinciall Synod held, nor Spiritual Courts erected, nor the Canon Lawes accepted, nor ordinary or other Ecclesiastical persons admitted (as such), nor Catholic religion publickly allowed; and whereas three partes of the people or foure (at least) are hereticks, I desire to be resolved:

I°. Whether a lay Catholick can, with a safe conscience take charge or government or of an office in such a country as this, where he may not, nor dare discharge all the dutys and obligations of a Catholick Magistrate, nor yeald and mayntaine to the Church, all her rights and liberties which Shee hath in other Catholick Countryes?

II°. Whether the lay Catholickes (in such a country as this) are bound to accept or admitt of all the Canon law, and *in* speciall of the Councill of Trent (extra sidem) or whether the Canon law (or such) binds in this country, afore it be accepted by some law or custom.

III°. Whether the exemptions of the clergy for their persons, lands, goods, Tennants Domestiques, or privilege of Sanctuary to theyr houses, or Churches, etc. are due to them of Divine right, by immediate grant from Christ to his Church, so that Princes becoming Christians, were instantly obliged in conscience to allow and confirme those exemptions, or at least to permit and suffer the Church to practice and enjoy them, or whether they hould them of the free and voluntary guift and devotion of pious princes, and States, so that in a countrey newly erected, on becoming Xtian, a grant or charter from the Prynce thereof of such libertyes, and exemptions, is necessary before the clergy of such a country can clayme them as theyr right, and due in point of conscience, and whether before such a grant admittance or allowance of their Priviledges, may the state practice contrary to them without sacriledges, or incurring the censures Bullæ Cœnæ.

IV°. Whether houlding of Courts with external co-ercive iurisdiction, be a part of the powers of the Keys left by Christ to his Church, or whether it be a part of the sword, put by God into the hands of Princes, and from them granted unto spiritual ordinaryes; and where Ecclesiastical Tribunals are here to be erected, with such power of external co-ercive jurisdiction, may the Prynce erect them by his own charter, or must it be done by special commission and delegation of the See Apostolique?

V°. Whether the conusance of causes testamentary, belong to the Spirituall Court out of the nature of the causes themselves, and of the Churches' proper right, so that Xtian Prynces had no rightfull powere to heare and determine them, or whether Princes becoming Christian, did of theyr voluntary election sever theyr causes from theyr crown, and commit them to the spirituall ordinaryes, in consideration of some connexion and dependance which those causes have with some part of Xtian Doctrine, which must be sought from the mouth of the Priest, or in presumption of theyr faithfulness in discharging of their trusts?

VI°. Whether in such a countrey as this, may lay judges being Catholique by commission from the Lord Proprietary, or appointment of the law of the country, prove Wills, and committ administrations of the goods of the deceased, intestate, or whether they must have an intention to do it as delegated of the Sea Apostolique, and are obliged to endeavour with effect to procure such delegation or else incur the censures Bullæ Cænæ.

VII°. Whether in such a country as this, may a Catholique refuse to prove and record a will for this reason, because it giveth legacyes for masses to be sayd for the soule of the deceased, and conteynes in it the profession of the Testator, to dye a member of the Roman Catholique Church, out of which there is no salvation with other passages contrary to the religion of England, or whether is he bound to prove it, though the Lord Proprietor may incur danger for such a record?

VIII°. Whether Catholiques being members of the General Assembly in such a country as this may consent to the making of laws touching causes testamentary and namely to a lawe which shall appoint the residue of the estate of the deceased persons after all debts discharged, and legacyes payed to be employed to publick uses of the State, and not to pious uses as it is in the other Catholique Countryes?

IX°. Whether Catholiques being members of the General Assembly in such a Country as this, may consent to a lawe prohibiting the bequeathing or otherwise aliening of any fee to spiritual persons or religious houses, without leave of the Prynce, and voiding all guifts and alienations made otherwise?

X°. Whether a Catholique Executor or Admor, in such a Country as this, may observe the order of administering the goods of the deceased, used and prescribed in England (viz: to discharge first the debts, due to the Prynce, then executions, then judgments, &c.) or whether he is bound to observe ordinem restitutiones delivered by Casuists (as Bonacina and others) viz: to discharge first the debtes due to Spirituals and after, lay debtes, in *ordineris*[1] and whether a Catholique may refuse such an illegal account and compel the Executor and administrator to satisfy creditors according to the laws of Eng^d?

XI°. Whether may Catholiques being members of a Generall Assembly in such a country as this consent to lawes touching causes matrimoniall, as to appoint the publishing of banns (for politique considerations), and to prohibit marriage without such banns published, or license obtained from the Commissary being lay, or to limit the degrees of consanguinity within which marriage shall not be contracted, or for the tryall and determinings of causes matrimonial, or whether may a Catholique being lay under the Prynce, State, grant licenses of marriage, and by commission from the Prynce try and determine such causes according to the lawe of the country, or in defect thereof according to the common law without the incurring the censure B. Ca?

XII°. Whether may Catholiques being members, &c., consent to a lawe prohibiting the marriage of apprentices without the consent of theyr masters or miss^{ts} and imposing penalties upon

---

[1] The MSS. is imperfectly transcribed.

the Priest solemnizing, &c., and whether such a law be against liberty of marriage?

XIII°. Whether may Catholiques being members, &c., consent to a lawe which for publique custom barrs the female from inheriting, or houlding of lands, unless they marry within a time limited (only leaving them a liberty to sell or dispose thereof to theyr best advantage), and is such a law against conscience?

XIV°. Whether land granted by the Lord Proprietor, to religious persons by the ordinary and common conditions of plantations, doth eo ipso (because granted to religious) become spiritual fee, and exempt from laica onera?

XV°. If a trespass be pretended to be committed upon the lands held by Religious Persons, whether may the Religious, without trying the trespasse in some Court (spiritual or temporal), proceede against the pretended trespasser, by putting in force against him the censures Bullæ Cœnæ? And whether by such declarations, the party be really and to all spiritual effects involved in the censures, afore to be adjudged a trespasser upon theyre land in some Court?

XVI°. When grants of lands, made by the Prynce to several persons lay and religious, are found prejudiciall to the publique, and fit to be reformed, whether may Cathls — being members of &c. consent to a law reforming all such grants? And whether may such a general lawe include the grants made to the religious; and whether may the Prynce, by virtue of such a lawe, resume or reform such grants made to them afore, or with a voluntary surrender of them by the Religions?

XVII°. Whether in such a country as this, may the Prynce or secular Judge, being a Catholique, summon Eccl[l] persons to the General Assembly, or draw them into secular Courts, where they are defendants in actions of debt, trespass, &c. & may he give sentence therein, as lawful Judge, and execute it upon theyr persons, lands, &c. without incurring the censures of Bullæ Cœnæ?

XVIII°. Whether may the secular Judge, being a Catholique, proceed to the trial and punishment of clerks being in orders, for any offence against the peace &c. of the Lord Proprietor, or for capitall cryme extending to the losse of life, or members without incurring, &c.

XIX°. Whether may Catholiques, being &c. consent to lawes imposing generall contributions towards publick charges, for the necessary support of the Prynce, or defence of the Country, and whether are spirituall persons, their lands, &c., included (for want of exemption)? And whether may the secular Judge, being Catholique proceed against such spirituall persons, &c., or religious houses, (without special and expresse licence from the Sea Apost.) or may he accept such imposition from such spirituall persons voluntarily without incurring, &c?

XX°. Whether the representative body mett in generall assembly, may make laws to dispose of the interests of particular persons, as of Clergymen, not being present, nor having proxies in such assembly, (tho. lawfully summoned thereto), nor otherwise holding Synods Provinciall, wherein theyr consents to such laws might be expected, and whether are such lawes against conscience.[1]

These "twenty cases," it will be perceived, amplify the points stated by Lewger, and proposed for solution, questions of the gravest importance to the Colony. They were forthwith forwarded by Father More to Rome for answer, and laid before the Sacred Congregation for the Propagation of the Faith, accompanied with the following memorial:[2]

---

[1] Stonyhurst MSS, Anglia, vol. iv., No. 108k.
[2] Records English Provinces, vii., p. 363.

" The Provincial of the Society of Jesus, in England, humbly represents to your Eminence that in the month of June, 1632, the King of England granted to the noble Baron of Baltimore, a Catholic, in propriety, a certain Province on the sea coast of North America, inhabited by infidels, which is this day called the Land of Mary, or Maryland, after the reigning Queen of England. The said Baron immediately treated with Father Richard Blount, at that time Provincial, at the same time writing to Father General, earnestly begging that he would select certain Fathers as well for confirming the Catholics in the faith, and converting the heretics, who were designed to colonize that country, as well for propagating the faith among the infidels and savages. The affair was surrounded with many and heavy difficulties, for *in leading the Colony to Maryland, by far the greater part were heretics, also the country itself a meridie Virginiæ ab Aquilone*, is esteemed to be a New England, that is two provinces full of English Calvinists and Puritans; so that not less, nay, perhaps, greater dangers threaten our Fathers in a foreign than in their native land of England. Nor is the Baron himself able to find support for the Fathers, nor can they expect sustenance from heretics hostile to the faith, nor from the Catholics, for the most part poor, nor from the savages, who live after the manner of wild beasts."

" The zeal of the said Father Provincial conquered these and other difficulties, and at first two Fathers were sent out, as it were, to explore and ascertain if there might be any hope of the gain of souls when the country should appear 'white to the harvest.' Some years ago, a geographical description of this country was presented to his Eminence, Cardinal Barberini, Protector, with an humble petition that he would deign to receive the Fathers sent out there, under the patronage of his kind protection, equally with the rest in England, so that the matter might be transacted in the most secret way, and without offence to the State of England. After this the fathers indeed increased both in numbers and in courage, in hunger and in want, in frequent diseases, which were fatal to some, and lastly, through various dangers, applied themselves with constancy to the salvation of souls, learnt the savage language, which is composed of various dialects, composed a dictionary, a grammar, and a catechism for the use of the infidels, and the divine goodness was pleased, so to favor these attempts that, beside others, a certain Emperor, having many tributary kings under him, with his wife and family and some of his ministers were brought to the faith, and unless hindered, '*a domestices fidei*,' a great door was laid open to the gospel. These impediments, and severe ones, did indeed arise, and from those from whom they were the least due.

" For since the said Baron was unable to govern Maryland in person, he appointed as his substitute a certain Mr. Lewger, his Secretary, who was formerly a minister and preacher, and being converted to the faith, retained yet much of the leaven of heresy, for he still maintained those dogmas so justly offensive to Catholic ears — that no external jurisdiction was given by God to the Supreme Pontiff, but merely an internal one *in foro conscientiae*; that no immunity for goods or persons, was due to him, or any other ecclesiastics, except such as lay princes and seculars chose to confer upon him or them; that it would be a great offence, to be mulct by punishment, to exercise any jurisdiction whatsoever, even of absolving from sins, without special license from the Baron, from whom all lawful jurisdiction was derivable. That a virgin, making a vow of virginity, and not marrying after the twenty-fifth year of her age, could not hold lands by heirship, coming from her parents, but that they must be sold, and if the partie refused to do, then by compulsory sale. That the General Assembly or Parliament possesses so great an authority over the property of all, that it could disposses every one it chose of their all, even to the under garment, for the use of the Republic, and other such like propositions of the said Mr. Lewger are comprehended in 20 questions which are laid before this Sacred Congregation by the hands of the Secretary.

"Therefore this Secretary, having summoned the Parliament in Maryland, composed with few exceptions of heretics, and presided over by himself, in the name of the Lord Baltimore himself,[1] he attempted to pass the following laws, repugnant to the Catholic faith and ecclesiastical immunities: That no virgin can inherit, unless she marries before 29 years of age; that no ecclesiastic shall be summoned in any cause, civil or criminal, before any other than a secular judge; that no ecclesiastic shall enjoy any privilege, except such as he is able to show *ex Scriptura*, nor to gain anything for the Church, except by the gift of the Prince, nor to accept any site for a Church or Cemetery, nor any foundation from a Convert Indian King, nor shall any one depart from the Province even to preach the Gospel to the Infidels by authority of the See Apostolic, without a license from the laye Magistrate; nor shall any one exercise jurisdiction within the Province which is not derived from the Baron, and such like.

"The Fathers of the Society warmly resisted this foul attempt, professing themselves ready to shed their blood, in defence of the faith, and the liberty of the Church — which firmness greatly enraged the Secretary, who immediately reported to Baron Baltimore that his jurisdiction was interrupted by the Fathers of the Society, whose doctrine was inconsistent with the government of the Province. Hence, the said Baron, being offended, became alienated in his mind from the Fathers of the Society of Jesus, and at first, *ipso facto*, seized all their lands, and let them to others, as though he were the Lord and proprietor of them, although King Patuen had given them the same lands, when he was a catechumen, upon the express condition for supporting priests, who had brought his subjects to the true knowledge, faith and worship of God. The said Baron, with others favourable to his opinions, began to turn his attention to the expulsion of the Fathers, and the introducing others in their stead, who would be

---

[1] This must refer to the General Assembly of October, 1640.

more pliable to his Secretary. Therefore he procured last year, to petition the Sacred Congregation of the Propagation of the Faith, in the name of the Catholics of Maryland, to grant a Prefect and priests of the secular clergy, faculties for the same mission, making no mention in the meantime, of the labours of the Fathers undertaken in that harvest, nor expressing the motives which induced him to substitute new priests. And in order that he might have some new grounds to urge for calling away the Fathers of the Society from thence, he proposed certain points, similar to those laid before the Sacred Congregation, to be presented to the Provincial by the hands of the Secretary, that he might subscribe them in the name of himself and of the Fathers in Maryland.

"But the Sacred Congregation, being entirely ignorant of these matters, granted the Petition; and in the month of August, 1641, faculties were expedited from the Sacred Congregation, and were transmitted to Dom Rosetti, now Archbishop of Tarsus. But since, perhaps, either the Prefect is not as yet appointed, or the faculties delivered, but are as yet, it is hoped, in the hands of Father Phillips, the Confessor of the Queen of England, the said Provincial humbly begs of your Eminence to deign to direct that the said faculties may be superceded if the matter is yet entire, or if by chance the faculties are delivered, that the departure of new priests may be retarded for so long as to allow the Holy See to decide upon what is best to be done for the good of souls.

"The Fathers do not refuse to make way for other labourers, but they humbly submit for consideration, whether it is expedient to remove those who first entered into that vineyard, at their own expense, who for *seven years* have endured want and sufferings, &c.; who have lost four of their own *confreres*, labouring faithfully unto death; who have defended sound doctrine and the liberty of the Church, with odium and temporal loss to themselves; who are learned in the language of the Savages, of which the priests to be substituted by the Baron Baltimore are entirely ignorant, and which priests either allow or defend that doctrine from which it must needs be that contentions and scandals should arise, and the spark of faith be extinguished, which begins to be kindled in the breast of the infidels.

"Nevertheless, the Fathers profess themselves ready, with all submission, either to return to England, from Maryland, or to remain there and to labor, even to death, for the faith and the dignity of the Holy See, as may seem fit to the prudence, the goodness and charity of your Eminence.

"And may God," &c.[1]

The exact method of the settlement of this dispute about the supremacy of the ecclesiastical or of the temporal jurisdiction does not appear. The results of it are manifest and are duly recorded.

Father Henry More, then Provincial of England, was a man of learning, wisdom, and imbued with a genuine love of English institutions. As far as in his power, he promptly settled all questions submitted to him, and gave a certificate that the Conditions of Plantation, with the annexed oath, were not contrary to the provisions Bulla de Cœna Domini. His certificate was as follows:

I ...., the Provincial of the Society of Jesus in the Anglican Mission, have read the Conditions of Plantation, and the oath above mentioned, nor do I find anything contained in them, nor in any part of them, that can render the most Illustrious Lord Cecilius, Baron of Baltimore (because he has imposed such

---

[1] Stonyhurst MSS. Anglia, vol. iv., 108k.

conditions or oath), or any of his officials, (because he publishes, executes or records them; or any of them, from his command) or any other person, or persons, (because they accept, or admit the said conditions, and oath, or any of them), respectively within the province of Maryland, subject to any censure of excommunication of the Bull Cœna, or the same persons or any of them guilty of any crime on this account.

In faith of which I have hereunto affixed my signature.[1]

The Provincial also executed a release in full of all lands acquired, and of all right to acquire, lands from Indians, and conveyed to the Proprietary the estate of Mattapany, granted to the Society by King Pathuen, the Manor of the Immaculate Conception and that of St. Gregory, and all other domains held in the Province, either by Indian grant or by grant to any person for the use of the Society.

This release is as follows:

TO ALL WHO SHALL READ, HEAR OR SEE THESE PRESENTS.

I, ..., the Provincial of the Society of Jesus in the Anglican mission wishes eternal salvation in the Lord. Since I have been informed that some one or more of our aforesaid Society have accepted, admitted, purchased or in some other way obtained for pious or other uses certain properties (fundos), tenements or inheritances in the Province of Maryland, situated within the limits of America, from some Indians or some person or persons, to whom no legitimate right or judicial power, derivable from them, was granted by any concession or concessions of the most

---

[1] Stonyhurst MSS. Anglia, vol. iv. This certificate in Latin is appended to the Conditions of Plantation and Oath in Latin.

Illustrious Cecilius, Baron of Baltimore, the Lord and Proprietary of the said Province: and that some one or more of our said Society, have actually taken, or would take possession of the aforesaid properties, tenements or inheritances, or of some part of the same, without any concession made by the aforementioned most Illustrious Baron under his great seal of the aforesaid Province; and by name, of some properties situated in a place that is called Mattapony or in some other place or places within the aforesaid Province: have even divided some of the said properties into various domains, which they commonly call signories or manors, and have called one of them the domain or manor of the Immaculate Conception, another of St. Gregory. Let it therefore be known to all that I, the aforesaid Provincial, for various honorable causes and reasons, as well for my own part as for that of my successors, and our aforesaid Society, do by these presents concede, transfer, resign, and remit unto the aforementioned Cecilius, Baron of Baltimore, and his heirs, all right, title or interest of our said Society, of whatsoever kind or nature that right or title may be, in or to the aforesaid domains, properties, tenements or inheritances, within the aforesaid Province, to which we cannot derive or have any legitimate and judicial title, from or under any concession made by the aforementioned Baron of Baltimore, under the great seal of his most Illustrious Lordship of the aforesaid Province. So that henceforth it shall be lawful for the aforementioned Baron of Baltimore, or his heirs, or for any other person, or persons, for him or for them, in his or their name, to take possession, to hold, and to use, all the aforesaid domains, properties, tenements or inheritances, or any part of them quietly and peaceably for his most Illustrious Lordship or his heirs, notwithstanding any right, title or interest, which either I or my successors or our aforesaid Society or Church have or can pretend to have, in or to all of the aforesaid things, or any part of them. And moreover as well on my own part, as on that of my successors, and of our aforesaid Society, by these presents I renounce, resign, and remit to the aforementioned most Illustrious Baron, and his successors, any title, right, or name, or reclamation, (*repostulatio*) whatsoever, which either our Society, or any member of it, has directly, or indirectly, or can pretend to have, from any Indians, or from any other person, or persons, to any use, or uses, whatsoever, of any properties, tenements, or inheritances in the said Province, which were either conceded, or hereafter shall be conceded, by the aforementioned most Illustrious Baron, or his successors, to our aforementioned Society, or to any member of the same, or to any other person, or persons, in trust for our aforesaid Society, or member of the same: only excepting this only pure and sole right, title and interest which our Society can or will be able judicially to derive, to those things from or under any concession or concessions from the most Illustrious Baron or his successors, the Lords and Proprietaries of the aforesaid Province, under his or their great seal, then for the time being or existing.

In testimony whereof I have hereunto subscribed with my hand and affixed my seal.[1]

The Proprietary considered it necessary to settle all the questions at issue between the Society and himself, and he therefore submitted to Father More the following instrument, which he required him to execute, by which he renounced all claim on the part of the Society, to any exemption, and privilege, from the operations of the law of the land, and he particularly renounced the right to acquire lands from Indians, and specially acknowledged the power of the temporal authority to have exclusive jurisdiction

---

[1] Stonyhurst MSS., Vol. iv., No. 108g.

over matters testamentary and causes matrimonial.

POINTS prepared by the Illustrious Lord Baron of Baltimore, the subscription to which, he will exact of the Rev⁴ Provincial of the Society of Jesus in England, both in his own name, and in that of the Missionaries who are engaged in Maryland.

1. I, A. B., make known by these presents and declare that notwithstanding any other titles or pretended rights whatsoever, I will not permit any one of our body or Society living within the province of Maryland, either by himself or by his procurators, agents or servants, to negotiate with any Indian or Savage, to sell to the same or to buy from the same anything whatsoever, without a special license of the Baron of Baltimore, the Lord of the province, and of his Lieutenant, General, or other Governor for the time, to be expressed in writing, and subscribed by his hand, or by that of some one of them, and signed with his seal. And by this my attestation or declaration, I abdicate, put off, and renounce any right or title whatsoever, which any of our body or Society has or can pretend to have, to negotiate with the aforesaid Indians or Savages, or to sell to the same, or buy from the same, anything without such special license, as has been said before.

2. Moreover I declare that no one living within the same aforesaid province, (whether he be an Ecclesiastic or lay person) can or ought to buy directly or indirectly from any Indian, &c. or from any other person whatsoever, or receive or turn to his own use, any lands situated within the said province, unless such persons are such, as have a legitimate right, competent to themselves, and derived from some concession, fortified by the great seal of the province, from the Baron of Baltimore, or his heirs or from some other person claiming the right from the same, or by his means, or under him, by virtue of some concession signed by the great seal of the province, as has been said: so that all other

whatsoever purchase or acceptance or occupation of such lands is in itself, and shall be invalid and nulle. Moreover by this my attestation or declaration, I break, invalidate and annul all purchase, or acceptance whatsover of such lands, in any other way than the aforesaid, made or to be made, or received by any one of our community or Society.

3. Moreover I declare that all the acts of the General Assembly within the province of Maryland, for the better administration of the said province decreed, or to be decreed hereafter, by the citizens of the said province, or by those furnished with sense of the province and with their counsel, consent and approbation, or by the greater part of them, or by their delegates or deputies, and assented to and confirmed by the Baron of Baltimore and his heirs, the Lords and Proprietaries of the said province, according to the power and direction granted for this, to the said Baron of Baltimore by the letters patent of His Royal Majesty of England—that all such acts, I say, oblige all persons whatsoever, whether Ecclesiastics or lay persons inhabiting or remaining within the said province, so that they submit and conform to them under the penalties in said act expressed, or to be expressed. Moreover considering and attending to the dependence which the administration of Maryland has on the state of England, to which it should be conformed as much as possible, I declare that no Ecclesiastical person whatsoever, inhabiting or remaining within the said province, can or ought to pretend, or hope for more, or other privileges, exemptions or immunities for their persons, lands or goods, within the said province, than are granted by his Royal Majesty, or by any of his officials or magistrates, to similar persons in England, nor is the Baron of Baltimore, or any of his officials, though they be Roman Catholics, obliged in conscience to grant others to the said Ecclesiastical persons. Moreover I declare that any official, &c., of the said Baron of Baltimore, or of his heirs, the Lords and Proprietaries of the said province, can form and institute judicial process against such Ecclesiastical per-

sons aforesaid, that is against their persons, and what they hold within the said province for the administration of justice to any other person whatever, or for the assertion, preservation and maintenance of the rights, prerogatives and jurisdictions whatsoever, granted to the said Baron of Baltimore, or to his heirs, over the said province, and the people inhabiting, or dwelling therein, by the gracious letters patent of his Royal Majesty, and sealed with the seal of Great Britain. Equally and in similar cases the said officials can institute similar process against the persons &c. of any lay person, inhabiting or remaining in the said province, without on this account, committing any sin or incurring the censure of the Bull *Cœna*.

Moreover I declare that all testamentary causes, proofs, concessions, letters of administration, &c., licenses of matrimony and others, all mixed causes, which in other countries are heard by the Ecclesiastical tribunals, and until within the said province, some Ecclesiastical tribunal be constituted with the consent of the Baron of Baltimore, can be heard &c. by that official or those officials, although Roman Catholics, who shall be designated, and shall have authority, from the said Baron of Baltimore, or his heirs, from the Acts of the General Assembly, among the same decreed, or to be decreed. The same official or officials can moreover make, and execute, or take care to be made, or executed, all that they shall consider necessary, and requisite to the expediting of the said causes, for the better government of the said province, in the same manner, and as amply as any Judge, or Judges of the tribunal of the Prerogative in England, do or execute in England, without on this account incurring the Bull *Cœna* or committing any sin.[1]

Along with these papers, among the ancient manuscripts at Stonyhurst, from which the fore-

---

[1] Stonyhurst MSS., Anglia, Vol. iv., p. 108f.

going papers were taken, is the form of an agreement or Secret Treaty to be entered into between the Provincial of the Society, and his successors, and the Baron of Baltimore, and his heirs, and successors forever. The paper is as follows:

A FORM OF AGREEMENT between the Father Provincial of England, on behalf of himself and his successors, with the Lord Cecil Baltimore and his Heirs, Lords Proprietors of the Province of Maryland, containing seven clauses, of which the following is an analysis:

1°. Whereas the King of England, by way of renunciation and special favor, had granted by Diploma the said Province of Maryland, with royal jurisdiction therein, to the said Baron of Baltimore, by force whereof no subject of England, even a Colonist of Maryland, was capable of accepting, buying &c. any portion of Maryland territory unless by license of the said Baron or his heirs. And since the same Baron had incurred, and was still incurring, great expenses, and daily underwent many troubles and dangers, both of person and property, chiefly on account of propagating Christianity in those parts, without having as yet received any fruit, or temporal gain, who, however, had he failed in his protection of the Colony, it never could (humanly speaking) have lasted so long, &c. &c., therefore let no one of our said Society at any time, directly or indirectly, by himself or another, accept, buy, &c. any lands &c. in the said Province for any use whatsoever, of the grant or gift &c. of any one, whether Indian or any other person or persons, otherwise than of the lawful licence of the said Baron and his heirs, duly sealed with the seal of this Province. But if any one of ours shall so accept &c. of any lands &c. contrary to the tenor of these presents, such acceptance, purchase, &c. shall be adjudged, and shall be understood to belong to the said Baron and his heirs.

II°. Since by the laws and statutes of England no lands &c. can be given or conveyed to any person whatsoever, spiritual or temporal, for any *pios* or Ecclesiastical *usus* without the special Royal license (to which rule the said Baron, as far as possible for just reasons in Maryland, should acquiesce, and since the same Baron, for the support of Ours living there, hath granted no mean part in the partition of Maryland, none of Ours, by himself or by another, shall accept, buy &c. any lands &c. for his own use or for any pious prohibited and comprised in the Statutes called *Mortmain*, which are at this time in force in England, unless with the special licence in writing of the said Baron first obtained, under his hand and seal. But if any one of Ours, notwithstanding this my agreement, shall, either by himself or by another, so accept &c. (as above) then and in that case all such gifts, purchases &c. shall be adjudged, and understood to belong to the said Baron and his heirs.

III°. Since it is sufficiently clear that Maryland depends upon England, that it could not support itself, unless they frequently sent over supplies of necessaries, and since it is not the less evident that as affairs now are, that those privileges, exemptions &c. which are usually granted to Ecclesiastical persons of the Roman Catholic Church by Catholic Princes in their own countries, could possibly be granted here without grave offence to the King and State of England, (which offence however may be called a hazard, both to the said Baron and especially the whole Colony). Therefore none of our said Society shall apply by any spiritual authority, or in any other manner demand or require from the said Baron, or his heirs, or any of the Officials in Maryland, any privileges, exemptions &c. in temporal matters, except such as are publicly granted to the Society, or the Roman Church in England. Nevertheless with this caution, that neither the said Baron, or &c. on the petition of any Catholic, cause to be inflicted corporal punishment on any of *Ours* in this Province, which in any manner can derogate from the privileges &c. which are usually granted in Catholic Countries, regarding the personal punishment of Ours, unless by chance the offence be a capital one, in which degradation will attach.

IV°. That no Jesuit shall be sent to Maryland without the license of the said Lord Baltimore and his heirs having been first obtained.

V°. That if the said Baron or his heirs shall at any time wish that any one or more of our Society, already sent, or hereafter to be sent to Maryland, be removed, and shall signify the said desire to the Provincial of England, or to the Superior of Maryland for the time being, such removal shall be made within a year after such desire shall have been so made known, provided that the said Baron, or his heirs pay the expenses of the removal, to any place which the Provincial or Superior shall reasonably fix upon: If the said Prov^l or Superior shall refuse to do so, or the party desired to be removed shall decline to go, then power is given to the Baron and his heirs to remove the said recusant; if the Baron or his heirs shall for any ground of bad conduct, wish to remove one or more of our said Society from the Province of Maryland, and the party retires voluntarily, and without coercive measures, then the said Baron or his heirs shall pay to the party leaving, the sum of £20 sterling, either in money or its equivalent in goods, &c.

VI°. The Provincial agrees that all members of the Society in Maryland shall on every occasion, and by every means defend the rights of the said Baron Baltimore and his heirs, as their absolute and Liege Lords, and shall swear allegiance to him, and them, as in the form of oath there given.

VII°. Declaration that those presents made by due authority and under his hand and seal shall be binding on himself and his successors of the said Society, and that the things therein contained shall be observed by all of Ours in Maryland, according to the tenor and meaning thereof.[1]

---

[1] Stonyhurst MSS., Anglia, Vol. vi., No. 108h.

This proposed treaty offered to abandon all claims by the Society of Jesus.

1. To the right to acquire lands from the Indians, or from any one else, or to have lands held by any one for the use of the Society, without license from his Lordship.

2. To the right of exemption from the equal operation of the laws, and to any privileges or exemptions in temporal matters, with the proviso, that corporal punishment should not be inflicted on any of "Ours" by the temporal Courts, except in capital cases, that is, that the Jesuits should be entitled to the benefit of clergy in all misdemeanours, and felonies not capital.

3. And that the Proprietary should control the ingress, egress and sojourn of the members of the Society to, from and in the Province at his discretion.

Lord Baltimore certainly declined to sign this agreement. No secret treaty between the Baron of Baltimore, and the Provincial of Jesuits, could control or limit the legislative power of the freemen of the Province. They had the right to make all laws, with the assent of the Proprietary. It is true, that he could have refused his assent to all acts making ecclesiastics subject to the lay jurisdiction, or denying them the benefit of clergy in crimes not capital, but he was determined that the pretensions of the extension of the Canon Law to Maryland should find no countenance, nor ever have any ground whatever to rest upon. Whether the Provincial signed the renunciation required by the Proprietary, or not, we have no evidence. Considering the character of Father More, it is most probable that he did, and thus the whole claim of the extension of the Canon Law was definitely determined and abandoned.

A singular result of the claim, however, is found in the institutions of Maryland, which has existed from that time to this.

By the Bill of Rights, every gift, sale or devise of land, or gift or sale of goods or chattels, to go in succession, or to take place after the death of the donor or seller, for any religious use, without leave of the legislature is void. This statute of Mortmain is not in force in the other States.

Since Fathers White, Altham and Copley were excused from serving in the General Assembly of 1637, no priest or clergyman has ever sat in that body. And the Constitution has always made all Ministers and Preachers of the Gospel ineligible, an exclusion which exists in no other State.

Since the contention concerning the ecclesiastical jurisdiction over causes matrimonial, marriage is not a civil contract alone, but some religious ceremony must be superadded to the civil contract.[1]

Maryland is the only State of the Union which requires the sanction of the Church to create the status of marriage.

At this period the situation of the Proprietary was most embarrassing.

His representative, Lewger, was at issue with the Jesuits, on their claim of the supremacy of the Canon Law, and the institutions which Lord Baltimore had determined to found in Maryland were inconsistent with the existence, principles and methods of procedure, of that Code. But his colony had been undertaken with the advice, coöperation and support of the Society and its great heads in England and in Rome.

The population, overwhelmingly Protestant, were restless and dissatisfied.

The feuds at home, had extended to the Province, and jealousies and bickerings showed themselves.

On March 22, 1642, a petition was presented by the *Protestant Catholics* complaining against Mr. Thomas Gerard, for taking away the books out of the Chapel. Upon which charge, after due examination, the Assembly found Mr. Gerard "Guilty," and sentenced him "to return the

---

[1] Denison vs. Denison, 35 Maryland Rep., 361.

Books and to relinquish all title to them, or to the house, and pay a fine of 500 lbs. of Tobacco towards the maintenance *of the first minister as should arrive."* [1]

While his Province was thus torn by religious feuds between Lewger and the Jesuits, Roman Catholics and Protestants, civil war broke out between the King and Parliament in August, 1642.

On the 26th March, 1642-3, Baltimore was cited before the House of Lords and placed under bonds not to leave the kingdom.[2]

Thus pressed by the troubles at home, and the distracted condition of the Province, he was firm and faithful to his purpose and aspiration, and at this very time, he invited the Puritans of Massachusetts, to emigrate to Maryland, offering them lands and privileges, and "free libertie of Religion," but Gibbons, to whom he forwarded a commission, "was so wholly tutored in the New England discipline" that he would not accept the invitation.[3]

He reorganized the government in a manner that he hoped would settle the disputes in the Colony and produce peace. He issued new commissions to Governor, Councillors and Secretary,

---

[1] Assembly Proceedings, 1637-1658, fol. 166.
[2] Streeter, 200 Years Ago, page 29. Allen, 46.
[3] Bancroft, Hist. U. S., p. 190, ch. vii.

He sustained Lewger, by reappointing him Secretary and "Judge of all causes testamentary and matrimonial" within this Province. Cornwaleys, who was commissioned as of the Council, refused to be sworn in.[1]

The commission to the Governor, authorized him to assent to all such laws as the Governor should think proper, and which should be adopted by the freemen. The authority committed to Lewger, definitely disposed of the claim of ecclesiastical jurisdiction over wills and marriages.

After having thus fi... denied the pretensions of the Jesuits, t... the extension of the Canon Law, he may have considered it wise to select his officers in vie... ...tion. The new reorganization did not produce t... peace for which it was framed.

The parties in the Province evidently sympathized with those at home. Baltimore could not leave England in the perilous condition of affairs, and in April, 1643, Leonard Calvert, having appointed Giles Brent, Esq., Governor, went there to confer with his brother. While he was there, the Parliament appointed the Earl of Warwick, Governor-in-Chief, and Lord High Admiral of all the American Provinces, with power to appoint subordinate Governors, and

---

[1] Council Proceedings, 1636-1657, p. 68.

"chiefly to the preservation and advancement of the true Protestant Religion among the said planters."

The absence of Leonard Calvert was disastrous to the fortunes of the Province.

In January, 1644, Governor Brent seized Captain Richard Ingle, commanding the London Parliament ship "The Reformation," "upon high treason to his Majesty," thus committing the Provincial Government definitely to the royal cause.

Secretary Lewger was not in sympathy with any such course. His whole weight and influence were on the side of peace and neutrality. This is proved by a commission issued by him in June, 1644, to Captain Henry Fleet, to conclude a treaty of peace with the Indians.

Between him and Governor Brent, therefore, there was an irreconcilable feud, growing out of the different views held by them as to the civil war, and Lewger's course towards the Jesuits in Maryland. Accordingly, in August, 1644, the Governor suspended the Secretary from all his offices and authority. In the meantime, war raged at home. Marston Moor was fought and lost to the King in July, 1644, while Leonard Calvert was with Lord Baltimore in the south of England, at or near Bristol.

He hurried back to his Province, where he arrived in September, 1644. He brought with him new commissions for Governor and Council. Giles Brent, John Lewger, Thomas Green, Thomas Gerard and James Neale, Esq's., all Roman Catholics, were appointed Councillors.

Why Lord Baltimore should, at this time, have reorganized his Government, and placed it exclusively in the hands of Roman Catholics, no reason appears. It may have been on the basis of a projected arrangement in England between the Puritans, and the Roman Catholics, looking toward a larger religious toleration, in a Union against the Royalist cause and the Church of England. However that may be, the measure brought speedy disaster. In February, 1645, Captain Ingle returned, with "a party of 'rowdies' or marauders, and took possession of the government." The destruction of the records by him, has involved this episode in impenetrable obscurity, until the recent publications of the Jesuit records of Stonyhurst.

The annual letter from Maryland to the Father Provincial of England, contains an account of Captain Ingle's doings, and throws light on the motives of the actors. They carried off the Fathers to Virginia and to England, whence they returned in February, 1648. Among them were Fathers White and Fisher. The Fathers found their flock in a more flourishing condition than their oppressors and plunderers. The two following years were years of faction, turmoil, and trouble. Leonard Calvert, a refugee in Virginia, appointed Captain Edward Hill, a Parliamentarian, to act as Governor in his absence. Hill ordered an Assembly to convene.

Calvert returned in December, 1646, and drove out Ingle, and repossessed the government.

He permitted the Assembly called by Hill to meet and act, although composed entirely of the opposing party.

Such was the condition of affairs in Maryland in January, 1647.

Governor Calvert, at the head of a Roman Catholic Government, intended to be a compromise between the extreme pretensions of the Jesuits, and the conservatism of the English Catholics. The great majority of the people Protestant, and in sympathy with the Parliament. The Secretary, Lewger, trying to combine the party of the Parliament, and of the Papacy, into an opposition to the Jesuits.

In the meantime the crisis of the Royal government had passed in England. Naseby ended the struggle in June, 1645 — a few months after Ingle had seized the government of Maryland. The issues between the Long Parliament and the

---

[1] Record English Provinces S. J., vol. iii. p. 387.

New Model of the Army under Cromwell were gradually assuming shape.

The Parliament struggled for a State religion; the Army insisted on religious toleration.

Cromwell wrote before Marston Moor: "The State, in choosing men to serve it, takes no notice of these opinions. If they be willing faithfully to serve it, that satisfies." From the field of Naseby he wrote to the Speaker of the Commons: "Honest men served you faithfully in this action. Sir, they are trusty. I beseech you in the name of God not to discourage them. He that ventures his life for the liberty of his country, I wish he trust God, for the liberty of his conscience."[1]

In the law remodelling the Army, a clause was inserted to dispense with the signatures of the Covenant in the case of "godly men," and the New Model of the Army was thus formed on a principle of quasi-toleration.

III.

The position of the English Roman Catholics during the struggle had generally been in sympathy with the Parliament.

---

[1] Green's Hist. of English People.

The Roman Catholic Lords withdrew from the House of Lords in 1642, "in order," says Rapin, "to present aspersions upon the votes of that House,"[1] and from indifference to the Royal cause. Lord Clarendon says that many Papists espoused the cause of the Puritans, and entered the Parliamentary army, because they fully expected that if the Puritans succeeded, they would allow "Liberty of conscience for all religions," and that "the French Ambassador used his utmost endeavors to prevent the English Catholics from joining the King's army."[2]

And Rapin alleges that at the battle of Edge Hill, fought October 23, 1642, "several Papists were taken prisoners by the King's army, and some Popish priests found among the slain."[3]

The Irish Catholics and Irish Puritans appear to have formed a coalition against the Royal party, and the English Church. The Committee appointed by the Irish Parliament in 1640 to carry to England the remonstrance against the Earl of Strafford was composed "of virulent Papists and rigid Puritans."[4]

As the forces controlling and directing the Revolution developed themselves, it became appar-

---

[1] Rapin's Hist. of England, Vol. x., p. 85.
[2] Clarendon's Hist. Rebellion, pp. 251-367.
[3] Rapin, Hist., Vol. x., p. 116.
[4] Leland's Hist. of Ireland, Vol. iii., p. 62.

ent that the object of the Presbyterian leaders was to establish their religion, and oppress all others. The Independents took a firm stand for liberty of conscience, and the Roman Catholics were thus forced by the logic of events to take sides with them and with the Army, which was most vehement in its professions of liberality.

The principal Roman Catholic nobles, the Provincial of the Jesuits, and the Superiors of the Roman Catholic Orders or Societies in England were incessant in their efforts to arrive at some understanding with the Army. They understood that the force of the Revolution was in the New Model, and with it, therefore, negotiations were opened and pressed.

Among the archives at Stonyhurst is a report of these negotiations, and their result, made at the time to the Provincial, probably for the information of the General of the Society at Rome. It is entitled "What has been done by the Fathers of the Society, and how have they proceeded, to obtain liberty of Conscience for all Catholics throughout England."[1] It then proceeds to give a brief statement of the condition of affairs in England, and goes on:

"The opposite party (the Independents) began to lift its head, to hate the tyranny of the Presbyterians, to call their rule a tyranny

---

[1] Stonyhurst MSS.—Vol. Ang. Hist., 1615-1677.

and at last to contend for freedom of conscience, as for their altars and their hearths.

"The heads of the soldiery sided with the Independents, and did valiantly, and finally they got possession of the King. When well nigh all power was in their hands, and they began to lay the foundations of freedom of conscience, to the end that they might establish it more deeply and firmly, they began to draw to their side, with no obscure attempts, the Catholics, who had lately groaned under the most heavy yoke of servitude, and this from no favor toward the Roman faith, which they hated, but from their hatred of the penal laws, which formerly enacted against the Orthodox, strike them also, as not attending church, to which they are not willing to be compelled.

"Nor did the Catholics behave sluggishly, for with the hope of obtaining liberty also, they made trial of the dispositions of the soldiers, and a certain most Illustrious Baron sent privily among them, one who should follow the camps, and warily watch for favorable seasons of speech.

"When one and another laymen had tried this, one thing hindered, which either baffled or certainly delayed our hope, the many things objected against the morals, doctrine and faith of the Catholics, which an unlettered man could not resolve, therefore it was, that one of *Ours* was asked to give his help for the common good of the Catholics, and to uphold the cause, which it was hoped would bring to all Catholics, quiet and the enjoyment of conscience, and of all their possessions. Moreover, if this liberty were once granted, and the laws which deterred many from the Catholic faith rescinded, a wide door is opened to the conversion of all England. The matter being brought before the Vice-Provincial, and counsellors having been heard, it was thought good to designate Father N. N., a professor of theology, who should refute the objections to our faith, and doctrine, and explain it, when needful, to the soldiery. He, when he saw that he would have to deal not with any private soldier, but with those who had the management of military affairs (commonly called 'agitators' [*agitatores*]), appeared, though unwilling, at their assembly. He did, however, so appear, for at the first meeting he so satisfied the president in refuting objections, that in full Senate (I should more rightly say *plebiscitum*) when many things had been said on this side and on that, and had been answered by our theologian, they came, with none gainsaying, to the opinion that Catholics might be admitted to fellowship in the benefit, and to the privilege of liberty. Thus was said and done in the lower chamber [*subsellio*], but because it had to be referred to the upper, it brought only a fair dawning of our hope, not yet sunrise much less full day.

"Drawn on by this beginning of the matter, the Illustrious Baron, certain nobles eminent for their skill and prudence in the conduct of affairs, being also joined in counsel with him, wisely thought it well to proceed further and use the help of the theologian. So all thought it necessary, that the counsels of the Catholics and the wishes of the agitators or assistants should be imparted to the generals [*belli ducibus*], colonels [*chiliarchis*], and leaders of the soldiery, that is to say, to the council of war (by whose mind and opinion Parliament [*comitia publica*] was almost wholly swayed at this state of affairs). This was a more serious and difficult matter, for some, gaping after the goods of Catholics, which were now confiscated everywhere, seemed disposed to be subserving the avarice of the soldiers; they ill brooked that these should revert to their owners, and for themselves to be disseised of that prey. Others, from a hatred to the faith and a most wicked animosity against the Roman See, alleged many things which, as incompatible with the rule of the Independents, would disturb their Commonwealth. Here the theologian and the nobles had great labor [*lit.* "had to sweat"]. They promised that so far as the Commonwealth was concerned, all things should be undisturbed, that there was nothing in the faith and morals of Catholics which did not well agree with the commerce and society of the heterodox; whereunto Germany, Holland, and other provinces bear witness, where Catholics dwell in peace under the rule of others, enjoying liberty of conscience; finally, that they bound themselves to render all civil obedience to the King and magistracy; nor was this pledge made by the Catholics without consulting the King, that his majesty might suffer no detriment. The most factious could object nothing to this, save only that all Papists were slaves of the Pope, servile to his rule, everywhere serving his will, and so subject to his sway that they would make this pledge, and every compact entered into with the heterodox, would stand or fall, not otherwise than according to the Pope's will. That nothing certain or constant was to be looked for from those, who so stubbornly cling to the power and will of the Pontiff, and teach that faith is not to be kept with heretics.

Who does not see that these things were said from a desire of faction? So the Catholics urged in reply that the Papal power did not extend to things unlawful; that the Pope, without doubt, would consent to this pledge wherein the welfare of his flock is consulted, where the free exercise of their religion is promised, where all the laws offending against the faith are either silent, or are rescinded. Finally, if he should consent, he would not easily go back from his promise given, nor would he absolve those who had pledged their faith. This address was able to move some to assent, but was not able to influence all. It was therefore decreed that the Catholics should be admitted to liberty of conscience and the enjoyment of their goods on this condition and not otherwise — that they should affirm in writing, and in express terms, that the Pope could not invalidate this agreement made with them, nor absolve Catholics from its obligation."

These propositions were laid by the Roman Catholic nobles " before the heads of the Clergy and of the Religious Orders, declaring that on their solution depended not only their property, but liberty of conscience, the faith of many, and, under Providence, the conversion of all England."

Those authorities were unwilling to commit themselves or their laity on questions of Papal power without consulting the Pontiff himself, and no time was allowed for such a reference, and therefore they subscribed to a "formula," as follows:

"Relying upon what is said in the 12th proposal, printed August 1, 1647, by the authority of his Excellency, Thomas Fairfax, Knight — That all penal statutes which hitherto retain their force against Roman Catholics shall be revoked, and furthermore, that they shall enjoy liberty of their conscience by concession of Parliament, it shall be determined that it shall not be lawful for any person or persons, subject to the Crown of England to profess, or to recognize as true, or otherwise to persuade, these following propositions:

I. That the Pontiff has the power of absolving any person or persons from their obedience to the civil government established in this nation.

II. That it is lawful, by virtue of a command or dispensation of the Pontiff or the Church, to slay, destroy, or otherwise injure or offend any person whatsoever, because they are either accused, or condemned, or censured, or excommunicated on account of error, schism, or heresy.

III. That it is lawful in itself, or by the dispensation of the Pontiff, to break faith or oath, given to the aforesaid persons, for the reason that they have fallen into error or heresy.

After consideration of these promises, we sign upon another part of the page, that each of these propositions may be answered negatively, and the names of those subscribing are these:"

Here follows, with the names of the Superior of the Clergy in England, of the Benedictines, Carmelites, Franciscans, &c., those of Father Henry More, Provincial of England, and of Father George Ward, the Theologian of the Society.

This proposal was laid before Parliament and was rejected, and instead thereof these offers, as a basis of religious toleration and liberty of conscience, were adopted by the House:

"PROPOSITIONS to be offered to Catholics, or conditions to be observed by them, if they desire to enjoy the general liberty of conscience:

1. That no Catholic shall bear arms.
2. That they shall hold no office in the commonwealth.
3. That they may have the exercise of Religion privately, *only* in their own houses.
4. That it shall be held a capital crime if any one, by writing, printing, preaching or teaching, shall promulgate or persuade these following heads: —
    I. That it is lawful in itself, or by virtue of a dispensation of the Pope, not to keep a promise or oath with a heretic for this sole reason, that he is a heretic.
    II. That it is lawful, by precept, or dispensation of the Pope or the Church, to slay, destroy, or otherwise injure or damage any one, for the reason that he is accused, condemned, censured, or excommunicated, on account of error, schism, or heresy.
    III. That the Pope or the Church has the power of absolving from the obedience to be shown to the civil magistracy, when and so long as the persons who might be absolved enjoy the common laws and liberties of the nation.

5. That it shall be a capital crime if any Roman Catholic has intelligence with any foreign State or person whatsoever, hostile to this nation, concerning the public affairs thereof.

6. That the revocation of the penal statutes shall only extend to native subjects of this nation.

The kind of liberty of conscience offered by these propositions was not what the Roman Catholic nobles and clergy were striving for. The overthrow of the Presbyterians, and the ascendancy of the Independents, in the Parliament put an end to all desire on the part of the latter, for toleration in matters of religion. We do not know who "the Most Illustrious Baron" was, who was the leader and director of the negotiations, with the army of Cromwell, above described. Inasmuch, as Cecil Calvert was at that precise time, enforcing the largest toleration in Maryland, and inasmuch as he was in close and constant communication, with Henry More, the Provincial of England—and it appears that the "Baron" invoked the assistance of the Jesuits in those negotiations—there are some grounds for the surmise, that the nobleman referred to was the Baron of Baltimore. Whether that be so or not, it is certain that no such movement could have taken place among the Roman Catholic nobles at that time, without Lord Baltimore being a party to, and participating in it.

The general and profuse professions of the Independents, in favor of liberty of religion, as long as they were in the minority, appear to have deluded the Roman Catholics then, as they have misled Mr. Gladstone in these latter days. It is true, as he states, that the House of Commons did, in October, 1645, pass an order declaring that the inhabitants of the Summer Isles should enjoy freedom of conscience in matters of religion. Their proposition for liberty of conscience as above formulated to the Roman Catholics, was the only sound which they ever made, from which the statute of toleration of Maryland could have been "an echo." The moment they secured power in England, and in Maryland, they signalized it by the bitterest intolerance.

Therefore it does not seem that "the Maryland statute was 'an echo' of a British ordinance of 1647 and a resolution of the House of Commons of 1645."

In June, 1647, Leonard Calvert died in Maryland, after having appointed Thomas Green, a Roman Catholic, to act as Lieutenant-General and Governor, until a successor should be legally commissioned.

The following summer of 1648 not only decided the fate of the Royal cause in England, but determined that the Army would control the Parliament. With the destruction of the monarchy accomplished, and the creation of a military government, imminent and inevitable, it would have been madness for Lord Baltimore, to have attempted to retain his Roman Catholic government, in the Province. Governor, Secretary and Council were all of that faith.

Since 1643, he had retained control of his province, in the face of the ordinance appointing the Earl of Warwick, Governor General. In 1646, his brother had driven out Ingle, the Parliamentarian, and it was absolutely necessary

First. That the provincial organization should be placed in harmony with the powers controlling England.

Second. That Roman Catholics should be protected from the overwhelming force now arrayed against them, and

Third. That the dissensions and quarrels within the Province itself, should be composed, that the Jesuits should be satisfied, that the Protestants should be contented, and that all should be quieted.

Peace and order, contentment and happiness in Maryland, in accord with the situation of affairs in England, were the conditions to be accomplished, by wise statesmanship, and courageous and prompt action.

In these trying circumstances it was necessary for Lord Baltimore to have the sympathy and advice of the very ablest friend, the assistance of the very wisest counsellor, and the support of all such persons in authority, as would be willing to aid him. He spent the entire summer of 1648 in digesting and maturing a complete re-organization of government, on principles which would satisfy all reasonable demands, and would compose the factions in Maryland.

He appointed a Protestant government, consisting of a Protestant Governor, William Stone, and three Protestant Councillors, Price, Hatton and Vaughan, with two Roman Catholics. Thomas Green the old Governor, and John Pile Stone was commissioned Governor, Lieutenant General, Chancellor, and Chief Justice;[1] Thomas Hatton, Secretary and Judge in causes testamentary and matrimonial; Captain John Price, Muster Master General; and Robert Vaughan, Commander of Kent.

Thus the complete control of the Province was passed over to the Protestants.

John Lewger was entirely excluded, and the Jesuits thus propitiated.

Religious toleration was secured to all, and especially to the Roman Catholics, by the new commissions, and the new oaths of office, and Mr. Secretary Lewger himself satisfied, by a rigid

---

[1] See Appendix E.

enforcement of the statutes of mortmain, in the new Conditions of Plantation.

The measures thus matured, consisted of Commissions, official Oaths, Conditions of Plantation, and a body of sixteen laws, which, when enforced and adopted by the freemen, would secure to them and their posterity forever all the rights and franchises, liberties and guarantees of Englishmen, many of which were then lost in England. With these rights, was the right of liberty of conscience, to all Christian people.

These measures were prepared on deliberation, and are dated at Bath, in the summer of 1648. They were intended by Calvert to be perpetual.

The Code of sixteen laws were "*proposed*" *to him* by some one, as a basis of settlement, and approved by him, as we shall presently see.

The policy of the Proprietary is expressed by the changes made by these official papers. Whereas the commissions of 1642 and 1644, authorized the Governor to assent to laws, in the name of the Proprietary, this commission expressly prohibited him from assenting to any laws, which may in anywise *concern religion*, without special and further warrant from time to time, under the hand and seal of the Proprietary. The oaths prepared for the officers of State and the Councillors were especially significant. While Cromwell, Sir Henry Vane, and the New

Model, the party of freedom of conscience in England, were professing the most earnest desire for religious toleration to all Christians, Baltimore knew that no confidence was to be placed in their professions. He embodied the principles they were so strenuously asserting in the commissions and oaths sent out to be taken in Maryland.

Those required of the Governor and Council contained this affirmation:

"I do further swear that I will not by myself, nor any person, directly nor indirectly, *trouble, molest or discountenance any person whatsoever, in the said Province, professing to believe in Jesus Christ, and in particular no Roman Catholic, for or in respect of his or her religion, nor his or her free exercise thereof within the said Province,* so as they be not unfaithful to his said Lordship, or molest or conspire against the civil government established here under him."

And added to the above, in the oath of the Governor, was this remarkable clause:

"Nor will I make any difference of persons in conferring offices, rewards or favours proceeding from the authority which his said Lordship hath conferred upon me, as his Lieutenant here, *for or in respect of their said religion* respectively, but merely as I shall find them faithful and well deserving of his said Lordship, and to the best of my understanding, endowed with moral virtues and abilities, fitting for such rewards, offices, or favours, wherein my prime aim, and end from time to time, shall sincerely be the advancement of his said Lordship's service here, and the public unity and good of the Province, without partiality to any, or any other sinister end whatsoever, and *if any other officer, or person whatsoever, shall, during the time of my being his said Lordship's Lieutenant here, without my consent, or privity, molest or disturb any person within this province professing to believe in Jesus Christ, merely for or in respect of his or her religion, or the free exercise thereof, upon notice or complaint thereof made to me, I will apply my power and authority to relieve and protect such person and to punish the persecutor,*" &c.

The new Conditions of Plantation declared that the Proprietary intended that

"No corporation, society, fraternity, guild, and body politick, as well spiritual as temporal, should have any benefit from said conditions, to inherit, possess, or enjoy any land within the Province, in their own names, or in the names of any other persons whatsoever, to the use, or benefit of such corporation, &c. Nor should any person having land, assign the same to such corporation, &c., or to any person in trust for them, to any uses forbidden, in any of the statutes of mortmayne,[1] heretofore made in England before the time of Henry VIII, without special license first had and obtained, under the hand and seal at arms of his Lordship, upon pain of forfeiture of all such lands.[2]

With the "sixteen laws" was sent a commission which explains that they

"Are written on three sheets of parchment, each sheet being signed by us, and all three together jointly with these presents,

---

1 Appendix on Mortmain, F.
2 Council Proceedings from 1636 to 1657, pp. 185, 196.

having the impression of our greater seal at arms, affixed unto them, which said laws *were proposed to us for the good and quiet settlement of our Colony and people of the said Province, and we finding them very fit to be enacted as laws,* do hereby consent that our said Lieutenant, William Stone, shall propose the said acts or laws hereunto annexed as aforesaid, to a General Assembly or Assemblies of the freemen of our said Province, or their deputies, and in case the said freemen or their deputies, or the major part of them, in any such General Assembly within our said Province, shall *within twelve months after the date hereof,* give their consent, that all and every of the said acts, or laws jointly contained in the said three sheets of parchment hereunto annexed, shall be enacted for laws within our said Province, by us, or our Lieutenant there for the time being, in our name, in such manner, and form, as they are written or drawn, without *any alteration, addition or diminution to them or any of them.*"[1]

All these measures of reorganization were entrusted to Thomas Hatton,[2] the new Secretary who was sent out with them, to put them in operation. He arrived at St. Maries in the winter of 1648-9. He took possession of the records on April 2, 1649, and his autograph receipt for them, as well as the subsequent record in his own handwriting, testifies to his fidelity to his duties as keeper of the records. No draft of the "Sixteen Laws" has as yet been found, but there is no difficulty in identifying them.

---

[1] Council Proceedings, 1636-1657, p. 209.

[2] Thomas Hatton was the grand nephew of Sir Christopher Hatton, Lord High Chancellor of Queen Elizabeth. Hanson's Old Kent, p. 113.

The General Assembly met on the 2d of April, 1649, and adjourned on the 21st of the same month. It passed twelve acts, of which the first nine were, on August 26th, 1650, assented to by the Proprietary.

Chapters 7 and 8 of those laws, relate to the planting of corn, and marking of hogs, and were certainly not prepared by the Proprietary, but were the work of the local legislators.

The other seven acts, were therefore among the "Sixteen Laws." As soon as the General Assembly met in April, 1650, "they read and considered the Sixteen Laws sent over by his Lordship, to be assented to, and enacted without alteration."[1]

They passed thirty-two acts, of which Chapters 23 to 31, inclusive, were assented to, together with the nine acts passed in 1649, by the Proprietary in one instrument on April 20, 1650.[2] The acts thus passed in 1649, and 1650, constitute the precise sixteen laws, proposed to, and accepted by the Proprietary, in August, 1648, as a basis of settlement.

They are:
1. The act concerning Religion.
2. Against counterfeiting the Great Seal.

---

[1] Assembly Proceedings, 1637-1658.
[2] Bacon's Laws, 1650. Assembly Proceedings, 1637-1658.

3. Against purchasing lands from Indians, which enforced the prohibition of the Conditions of Plantation, and the renunciation by the Provincial of the Jesuits, of the right thus to acquire lands.

4. Against sedition, and all who deny his Lordship's title and dominion.

5. Against Fugitives.

6. Against kidnapping Indians.

7. Imposing a tax of 10 shillings per 100 lbs. on all tobacco, exported in Dutch bottoms to any other than English Ports. This tax for the support of the Proprietary.

These were the laws passed at the session of 1649, part of the Sixteen Laws.

At the session of 1650 were passed:

8. An act recognizing the Proprietary's title by the laws of God and man, to this Province.

9. For amnesty and oblivion, for all participation in rebellion, between February 15, 1645, and August 5, 1646, excepting Richard Ingle and John Durford, mariner.

10. Against raising money by taxation, without the consent of the freemen in General Assembly.

11. That the freemen shall not be compelled to aid or assist with their persons or estates in the prosecution of any war, waged beyond the limits of the Province, without the consent of the General Assembly, and that Martial Law

shall never be declared, only in time of camp or garrison, and then only within such camp or garrison.

The tenth and eleventh acts are provisions of the Petition of Right,—3 Car. I, 1628.

12. Against exportation of his Lordship's ordnance, ammunition, goods, or cattle.

13. That the debts due the Proprietary, should be first paid.

14. Prescribing an oath of fidelity to his Lordship.

This act requires an oath to be taken by every inhabitant now in, or who shall hereafter come to the Province, swearing that "you will never deny, but will ever defend, and maintain his Lordship's rights under his charter, not in any ways understood to infringe or prejudice Libertie of Conscience in point of Religion."[1]

15. Providing for accountants to his Lordship.

16. That all inhabitants should have license to treat with Indians, and no persons not inhabitants to have such license.

The Act concerning Religion was the first act passed and was enacted on the 21st of April, 1649.

It is recorded in the handwriting of Thomas Hatton, the Secretary, and in the margin is the

---

[1] Lib. W. H. and L., fol. 10. Lib. C. and W. H., fol. 122.

entry that it was confirmed by his Lordship by his instrument under his hand and seal on the 26th of August, 1650, and the certificate signed with the autograph of Philip Calvert.[1]

The preamble of the Act sets forth:

"Forasmuch as in a well ordered and Christian commonwealth, matters concerning religion and the honor of God ought in the first place to be taken into serious consideration and endeavoured to be settled, therefore, &c."

It then imposes penalties for denying the three persons of the Godhead, or the Trinity, or using reproachful words concerning the Blessed Virgin Mary, the mother of our Saviour, or the holy Apostles, or Evangelists, or using opprobrious epithets towards persons, or in a reproachful manner calling any person residing or trading within the Province, Heretick, Schismatic Idolator, Puritan, Popish Priest, Papist, Jesuited Papist, Lutheran, Calvinist, &c., enumerating seventeen epithets, and names of sects, or religious denominations, "or other name, or terms in a reproachful manner, relating to matters of Religion," and for Sabbath breaking.

The act then sets forth this noble declaration:

"And whereas, the enforcing of the conscience in matters of religion, hath frequently fallen out to bee of dangerous conse-

[1] The original Lib. A., fol. 268, Council, &c., Proceedings, 1649-1650.

quence in those commonwealths where it hath been practised, and for the more quiet and peaceable government of this province, and the better to preserve mutuall love and unity amongst the inhabitants heere,

Bee it therefore also ordained and enacted, except as in this present act is before declared and set forth, that no person or persons whatsoever within this province, or the islands, ports, harbours, creeks, or havens thereunto belonging, professing to believe in Jesus Christ, shall from henceforth be any waies troubled, molested or discountenanced, for or in respect to his, or her religion, nor in the free exercise thereof, within this province, or the islands thereunto belonging, nor any way compelled to the beleefe or exercise of any other religion against his, or her consent, so that they be not unfaithful to the lord proprietary, or molest or conspire against the civill government, &c."[1]

This act was the performance of the pledge made originally by the Proprietary, in his first conditions of Plantations, for liberty of conscience. It carried into execution the proclamation made just after the settlement prohibiting disputes concerning religion, and it was the confirmation and ratification of both by the freemen in General Assembly convened.

We have thus recovered the precise basis of settlement prepared in 1648, and accepted by Lord Baltimore, and then proposed by him to the freemen of Maryland as an agreement of reconciliation and peace forever.

It was:

1. A Protestant government.

[1] Appendix G.

2. Oaths to be taken by the Governor, and Councillors, binding them not to molest any one on account of his religion, and particularly no Roman Catholic.

3. An oath of fidelity to his Lordship, to be taken by every one in the Province then or thereafter, not in any ways to be understood to infringe, or prejudice Liberty of Conscience in point of Religion.

4. A Commission to the Governor, prohibiting him from assenting to any law concerning Religion.

5. Conditions of Plantation, which prohibited any corporation spiritual or temporal, or any person to their use, from acquiring land in the Province, contrary to the Statutes of Mortmain.

6. The Sixteen Laws, to which he assented beforehand, which were, when passed by the Assembly, to remain in full force forever, and which were required to be enacted, without alteration or amendment.

If this settlement were accepted, the consequence would be, that the Protestant majority would be represented and protected by the Protestant government.

The Roman Catholic minority, would be made safe, by the Commission of the State officers, by their official oaths, and by the Acts of Assembly. The Jesuits would be guaranteed perfect security, and while the Statutes of Mortmain were enforced against them, and all persons were prohibited from purchasing land from the Indians, they secured the right to acquire land from the Proprietary, or with his consent, and license to trade with, and preach to the Indians. The Secretary, Lewger, was satisfied, because although in deference to the Provincial of the Society, he was left out of the new government, he had carried his point of prohibiting the Jesuits from acquiring land from the Indians, or of holding it, save with the consent of the Proprietary.

The insurgents of Ingle's Rebellion would be pardoned. The title of the Proprietary would be protected from domestic question or future denial. Supported by the consent of all the freemen, his property rights would be asserted and assented to, and the freemen themselves guaranteed and protected from illegal Subsidy, Aid or Tax, from Martial Law and from compulsory military service, save in defence of their homes, as guaranteed by the Petition of Right.

The entire settlement was further fortified by the oath of every person resident in the Province, reserving "Libertie of Conscience in point of Religion to himself and all other persons."[1]

---

[1] Act of 1650, ch. 29, The oath of fidelity. Bacon's Laws, 2 Bozman, 671.

These propositions are as wise, as statesmanlike, as far-reaching as any lawgiver ever propounded to any distracted society or faction-torn state.

The General Assembly met April 2, 1649, to consider them, Governor Stone presiding. They pondered them cautiously, adopted seven of them as we have seen, and on the last day of the session, April 21, "a letter to his Lordship was signed by the whole House present."[1]

In this letter they excuse themselves, for having adopted the Code only in part. They say:

"We have read, and perused, and debated, the body of laws prepared by your Lordship, to be assented to by us, as perpetual laws, but finding them so long and tedious, containing so many branches and clauses, we cannot, in justice to ourselves, and our posterity, concur in enacting them without further discussion, which we are now unable to give, because we are forced into a crop at this time of the year."

They further state, that inasmuch as he requires the whole body of the laws to be assented to, without alteration, they are not willing to adopt them entire. They have, therefore, decided to

"Reflect on such things as may give your honor, for the present, most satisfaction, which, if they mistake not, are chiefly four, to wit:

"That the country may be preserved with peace, and defended and governed with justice.

---

[1] Assembly Proceedings, 1637-1658, p. 339-351.

"2ndly. That some competent support may be raised to your Lordship, and your Lieutenant here. 3rdly. That a stock of cattle may be raised again for your Lordship, and 4th. That all should be satisfied who had concurred to the regaining of the country. To that end, we have first chosen and *selected out of all your Lordship's laws, such as seemed to us most conducive to confirm a long desired and settled peace among us.*"[1]

To this letter Baltimore replied at length, during the same year, and set forth his rights and claims under his charter. He says that "in the said body of laws there is provision made for *freedom of conscience*, *for freedom of taxes*, (but such as shall be laid by the Assembly's consent), for *freedom from martial law*, but only in time of camp or garrison, and within such camp or garrison, for *freedom from being compelled in any kind to contribute to any war* out of our said Province, without the consent of the Assembly, for *freedom of trade* with the Indians upon reasonable conditions," and he complains that some of them have "stumbled at" the title "absolute Lord and Proprietary" used in the laws and at the oath of fidelity provided by them to be taken... He shows that both are his right under the charter.[2]

From his language that they *were proposed to him* for the good and quiet settlement of his

---

[1] Assembly Proceedings, 1637-1658, p. 339. 2 Bozman, 665.
[2] Assembly Proceedings, 1637-1658, p. 351. 2 Bozman, 668.

colony: from the declaration of the Assembly that they selected such laws as would give him most satisfaction, first of which they think was that the country may be *preserved with peace, and defended and governed with justice,* and as they believed most *conducive to confirm a long desired and settled peace among us;* from his reply pointing out the wisdom and justice of the Code, which provided for freedom of conscience, freedom from taxes save by their own consent, freedom from martial law and from military service, or support of war beyond the province, and freedom of trade with the Indians, we must conclude that the Code of Sixteen Laws was prepared by some one in authority and proposed as a basis of settlement, and accepted by Lord Baltimore.

Mr. Gladstone says that:

"The Colonial Act seems to have been an echo of the order of the House of Commons at home, on the 27th of October, 1645, that the inhabitants of the Summer Islands, and such others as shall join themselves to them 'shall without any molestation or trouble, have and enjoy the liberty of their consciences in matters of God's worship,' and *of a British ordinance of* 1647."

It is true such an order was passed[1] on the petition of certain inhabitants of the Bermudas,

---

[1] On the 27th of October, 1645, in the Commons, "Upon the Petition of divers inhabitants of the Summer Islands:

"It is ordered, &c., That the Inhabitants of the *Summer Islands,* and such others as shall join themselves to them, shall without any Molesta-

or Summer Islands. An Independent Church or congregation, had been founded there.

The leading spirit in the movement was the Rev. Patrick Copland, who had been chaplain in the East India Company's service, and afterwards appointed Rector for a school, to be erected in Charles City county, in Virginia, for the conversion of the Indians, and the education of the people. When the Charter of the Virginia Colony was revoked, Copland proceeded to Bermuda, where, says Neill,[1] "on an isle of the sea, as suitable for contemplation as Patmos, he inclined to the simplest forms of worship consistent with propriety, efficacy and solemnity, and was convinced that the State should never interfere with any religious worship that did not disturb its peace, nor retard the prosperity of the commonwealth." He and his co-religionists organized a congregation, of which the officers were: Pastor, Rev. N. White; Elders, Rev. Mr. Golding and Rev. Pat-

---

tion or Trouble have and enjoy the Liberty of their Conscience in matters of God's Worship, as well in those Parts of Amiraca, where they are now planted, as in all other Parts of Amiraca, where hereafter they may be planted; until this House shall otherwise order. And

"It is further Ordered, that it be referred to the Committee of Lords and Commons for Plantations, to see this Order put in due execution."

Journals of the House of Commons [vol 4.] from December 25th, 1644 to December 4th, 1646

Printed by order of the House; passed May 31, 1712. Congressional Library. But the order of the House of Commons alone had no force, or binding effect as law.

[1] Neill's Colonization in America, pp. 179-80.

rick Copland; Deacon, Robert Cesteven, Esq., Councillor. The new church observed a weekly love feast, and used a catechism, prepared by Oxenstern, called "Milk for Babes." Copland, with his wife and others, soon seceded from this new church, and went to a small island of the Bahamas group, which he called Eleuthera, and whither he invited the Virginia non-conformists. They declined the invitation, and moved to Providence, on the Chesapeake, and the settlement of Eleuthera soon broke up.

The order of the House of Commons, therefore was that the New and Independent Church of the Summer Islands, should have and enjoy Liberty of Conscience. It was not intended by those who petitioned for it, nor by those by whom the order was passed, nor by the Committee for Plantations to whom it was referred, that any general Liberty of Conscience should be granted. On the contrary, it was expressly understood by all who adhered to the Puritan party, that all Papists and Prelatists were disturbers of the public order, and ought to be punished into renouncing their errors and sins.

No order for general liberty of conscience either in the Colonies or in England, ever was passed by the Long Parliament.

No such ordinance as that referred to by Mr. Gladstone was ever passed in 1647, or at any other time. None such is in Scobell's Collection of the Statutes and Ordinances of the Long Parliament.

Rushworth is given as authority for the alleged ordinance. Reference to his Collection shows that an ordinance for settling the government of the Church in a "Presbyterial way," was discussed in the Commons on the 6th of October, 1647, and an amendment was adopted for "giving ease to tender consciences of such as are Godly, and make a Conscience of their ways."[1]

On October 13, 1647, the Lords resolved, "That the King be desired to give his consent, and that all who do not conform, &c., shall have Libertie to meet for the service and worship of God, and so that nothing be done by them to the disturbance of the Kingdom."

On the same day the Commons resolved "That Liberty of Conscience or worship granted shall extend to none, that shall print, preach or publish contrary to the first 15 articles of the 39, except the Eighth, which mentions the three Creeds, made many years after the Apostles; that *nothing contained in this ordinance shall extend to any Popish Recusant, or taking away any Penal Laws against them.*"[2]

---

[1] Rushworth's Collection, vol. 7, p. 834.

[2] Rushworth's Collection, vol. 7, p. 849. This resolution of October 13, 1647, of the Lords, is quoted in full by Neill, Eng. Colonization, p. 285, as "that golden apple, the Ordinance of Toleration." It is the only order that can be found to support Mr. Gladstone, and it was promptly repudiated the same day by the Commons, as shown above.

On October 15, 1647, the Commons made this additional vote to their resolution of October 6:

"That the indulgence as to tender consciences, before mentioned, *shall not extend to tolerate the use of Common Prayer in any place whatsoever*."[1]

But even this Ordinance did not pass, and the record of the Long Parliament nowhere contains any act granting liberty of conscience to either Papists, that is, Roman Catholics, or Prelatists, that is, Churchmen.

On the 2d of May, 1648, it did pass the terrible ordinance "for punishing heresies and blasphemies." This fearful statute denounces the punishment of death against all who deny:

1. The belief in God.
2. The doctrine of the Trinity.
3. The dogma of Predestination.
4. The inspiration of the Scriptures.
5. That the Godhead and manhood of Christ are several natures.
6. That his manhood is pure and unspotted.

It punished with perpetual imprisonment, all who shall affirm:

1. That all men shall be saved.
2. That all men have free will.
3. That there is a Purgatory.

---

[1] Rushworth's Collection, vol. 7, p. 842.

4. That there is a rule of Faith other than the written law of God.

5. That the sacraments of Baptism and the Lord's Supper are not ordinances commanded by the word of God.

7. That Infant Baptism is unlawful.

8. That Church government by Presbytery is unlawful.[1]

This ordinance, it will be observed, created a test of Christian doctrine and punished all who refused to adopt such test.

It punished Churchman and Roman Catholic with death, for denying the dogma of Predestination, and the inspired authority of the Holy Scriptures, and it imprisoned for life all Baptists, all Universalists, all believers in Free Will, and all who denied the divine authority of government by Presbytery.

On the 9th of August, 1650, was passed another similar ordinance for "Punishment of Atheistical, Blasphemous, and Execrable Opinions."[2]

Notwithstanding the constant professions of Cromwell, Sir Henry Vane, the Council of Agitators and the New Model of the Army — the negotiation of the Roman Catholic Peers in 1647, under the direction of the Jesuits, for religious

---

[1] Appendix H.
[2] Appendix J.

toleration had been an utter failure, and they had been refused distinctly and emphatically. When, therefore, in the summer of 1648, it became manifest that the monarchy had fallen, and that the Parliament was controlled by a fierce and bigoted soldiery, the bloody ordinance of May 2 gave warning of what might be expected, and Baltimore may well have been appalled at the danger which threatened his family and friends in Maryland, and the free institutions he had labored so long to establish there.

In his Province, matters were if possible in a still worse condition.

Maryland, overwhelmingly Protestant and in sympathy with the Parliamentary party; religious toleration in England drowned in blood by the Ordinance of May 2, 1648; Ingle's rebellion smothered, not extinguished; the Jesuits claiming exemption from lay jurisdiction, and, as a consequence, the right to acquire land by independent title from the Indians; John Lewger, the Proprietary's Secretary and representative, exasperating every issue, by insisting that the Jesuits should be subject in every respect to the secular law, should be prohibited from exercising the discipline of the Society over its own members, or performing the sacraments of the Church without the permission of the temporal power; these were the circumstances facing Cecil Calvert, making the crisis of his life.

He needed then wise counsel, a courageous heart, and a sincere and faithful friend.

The planting of the Colony had been undertaken by the English Roman Catholics, under the advice and supervision of the Society of Jesus.

Father Richard Blount, Provincial of the English Province, representing the ancient houses which had adhered to the Church, as well as wielding the power of the Society, had as we have seen, sent out Father Andrew White and two other Jesuit priests with the first Lord Baltimore, first to Avalon, and thence to explore the country southward to find a place suitable for colonization.[1]

When the charter of Maryland was issued to the second Lord Baltimore, he had maturely considered all the objections urged to it, and had decided in favor of its practicability. Baltimore had also applied to the General of the Society, Mutius Vitelleschi, for advice and assistance, and by the direction of the General and the Provincial, Fathers Andrew White, John Altham and Thomas Copley accompanied the expe-

---

[1] Woodstock Letters, vol. 9, p. 158. Archbishop Carroll's narrative. "He had three priests with him in Newfoundland in 1629, and emigrated with his whole colony to Virginia." Doyle's English Colonies in America, p. 278–279.

dition "to attend the Catholic planters and settlers and to convert the Indians."[1]

Father Blount resigned his office of Provincial in 1635, and was succeeded by Father Henry More.[2] He was the great-grandson of Sir Thomas More, Lord High Chancellor of England in Henry VIII.'s time, illustrious for learning, piety, and patriotism, who had sealed with his blood his attachment to the old faith, and his defence of the right of conscience.

Father More was the historian of the Province, an office in the Society filled by its most able, pious and learned members.

He was Provincial, or Vice-Provincial, from 1635 up to 1647.

In 1647-48, he was Superior of the London District, or College of St. Ignatius, and the Vicar Apostolic of that district, became subsequently also Bishop of the Roman Catholics in the United States.[3]

From 1649 to 1652, and from 1657 to 1660, he was Rector of St. Omer's College.

He was the director of that movement made by the Roman Catholic peers, with the assistance of the Jesuits, in 1647, supported by the heads of the religious orders, to obtain concessions from

---

[1] Woodstock Letters, vol. 1, p. 3.
[2] Records of the English Province, Series iv, p. 421.
[3] Woodstock Letters, vol. 9, p. 165. Archbishop Carroll's Narrative.

the Long Parliament, whereby they might enjoy some measure of liberty of conscience.

In the dispute between Secretary Lewger and the Jesuits in Maryland, in 1639-40, he propounded the twenty cases of Canon Law to the Sacred College of the Propaganda for settlement and advice, and wrote the memorial, accompanying them, showing the injustice of the pretensions of the Secretary.

When Lord Baltimore in 1641 obtained permission to send the Jesuits home, he in 1642 prepared the second memorial to the Cardinal Prefect, and obtained a revocation of the order, so that some compromise might be agreed upon. If he did not prepare the articles of agreement, or the secret treaty, proposed to be entered into between the Society of Jesus, and the Barons of Baltimore, they were prepared with his knowledge and approbation. There is no doubt that he sought to have them executed.

He supported the Proprietary in his determination to exclude the Canon Law, as claimed by his subordinates in Maryland, and in enforcing the policy of the statutes of mortmain, and he executed the releases necessary to carry that policy out, and when the three propositions to Parliament in 1647, as a basis for obtaining civil and religious liberty were rejected, he, the head of the Society in England, familiar with the condition of Maryland, devoted to the principle of religious toleration, inherited from his illustrious ancestor, was of all men in the world, the proper person to be consulted by Lord Baltimore as to measures which should compose the difficulties between Protestant and Roman Catholic, between Jesuit and the Colonial authorities. His illustrious birth, his great authority, his known character and opinions, his efforts in favor of liberty of conscience, all point to him as the councillor and adviser of the Proprietary, in the difficult circumstances with which he was surrounded.

The great problem propounded to him by the Proprietary and by circumstances, was the preservation of the liberties of the province; of the rights of the Proprietary; of freedom of conscience; and the protection of the Roman Catholics and Jesuits from impending persecution. His solution of it was, the oaths, commissions and conditions of plantation, with the sixteen laws, to be passed without amendment or alteration.

First in importance of all these measures was the Act concerning Religion. If adopted, it would be a ratification by the freemen of the province of the original policy of the Proprietary on that subject. The ordinance of the Long Parliament of 1648, enforced conformity to the tenets of Puritanism under the penalty of death. The first section of the Maryland

Act of 1649, enforced conformity with the cardinal doctrines of Christianity, under the same penalty.

They are both laws to punish non-conformity.

But the first section of the Act, while in reality "an echo" of the ordinance, is inconsistent with the principles announced by the Proprietary in his first proclamation inviting settlers, as well as that made directly after the settlement, prohibiting "all unreasonable disputation in point of religion which tended to the disturbance of the peace and quiet of the Colony," and for infringing which, William Lewis was fined, and required to give security for his future good behavior, in 1638. It was most probably an amendment by the Assembly to the Bill sent out by Lord Baltimore. That amendments were made to these bills is certain.

Baltimore, in 1650, assented to the seven laws passed in 1649, and such assent was unnecessary, unless they had been amended, for he had agreed to them beforehand, if passed without amendment. In his letter to Governor Stone of August 26, 1651, he says expressly, that as to certain laws passed by the Assembly, "We for their full satisfaction sent last year, our assent *with such alterations as they themselves desired.*" [1]

---

[1] Assembly Proceedings, 1637 to 1658, p. 424.

The first section to enforce conformity, embodying a Puritan principle, enforced by the Ordinance of 1648, was therefore most probably an addition by the Assembly to the original draft. The remaining sections of the Act only carry out the policy of the proclamation against "unreasonable disputations in point of religion which tend to the disturbance of the peace and quiet of the colony."[1]

These provisions are but "an echo" of the laws of Utopia, as portrayed by Sir Thomas More.

That description "of the best state of a commonwealth" was intended to express the views of the philosophers of the New Learning, as to the principles which should control, and of the policy which should direct an ideal State.

It was an expression of the reflections of Erasmus and More, and of their conclusions as to what institutions would be best adapted to promote the welfare and happiness of mankind, and the strength and perpetuity of a people.

Under the guise of the description of the imaginary island of "Nowhere," More sets forth his ideas of the social economy, and of the political arrangements, necessary to constitute "the best commonwealth." It contains more than suggestions of social problems, hardly as yet settled, and still under discussion.

---

[1] Bozman, p. 674.

All citizens labored in Utopia, and none more than nine hours a day; slavery, except for crime or for prisoners taken in war, was prohibited; lawyers were not allowed. They abhorred war, and community of goods, of labor, and of meals was practiced. The religious institutions of the ideal State were exactly such as Baltimore founded in Maryland.

"There be divers kindes of religion, not only in sondrie partes of the Islande, but also in divers places in every citie. Some worship for God the sonne, some the moon, some some other of the planettes.

"They received the Christian religion with gladness, but they would not allow unreasonable disputations concerning it.

"They also, which do not agree to Christ's religion, feare no man frome it, nor speake against any man that hath received it, saving that one of our company, in my presence, was sharply punished. He, as soone as he was baptised, began, against our willes, with more earneste affection than wisdome, to reason of Christe's religion, and began to waxe so hote in his matter, that he did not onlye preferre our religion before al other, but also did utterly despise and condempne all other, calling them prophane, and the followers of them wicked and develish, and the children of everlasting dampnation.

"When he had thus long reasoned the matter, they laide hold on him, accused him, and condemned him into exile, not as a despiser of religion, but as a sedicious person, and a raiser up of dissention amonge the people.

"For this is one of the anncientest lawes amonge them, that no man shall be blamed for resoninge in the maintenance of his owne religion. For Kynge Utopus, even at the first beginning, hearing that the inhabitantes of the land were, before his coming thether, at continuale dissention and strife among themselves for there religions: perceving also that this common dissention (whiles every severall secte tooke several parties in fighting for there countrey) was the only occasion of his conquest over them al, as soon as he had gotten the victory. Firste of all, he made a decree that it should be lawful for everie man to favoure and folowe what religion he would, and that he mighte do the best he could to bring other to his opinion, so that he did it peaceablie, gentelie, quietly and soberlie, without hastie and contentious, rebuking and invehcing against other.

"If he could not by faire and gentle speeche induce them unto his opinion, yet he should use no kinde of violence, and refraine from displeasante and seditious wordes. To him that would vehemently and fervently in this cause strive and contende, was decreed banishment or bondage.

"This lawe did Kynge Utopus make not only for the maintenance of peace which he sawe through continuall contention and mutual hatred utterly extinguished; but also because he thought the decrie should make for the furtherance of religion. Whereof he durst define and determine nothing unadvised, he as doubting whether God desiering manifold and diverse sortes of honour, would inspire sundry men with sondrie kinds of religion, and this suerly he thought a very unmete and foolish thing, and a point of arrogant presumption to compell all other by violence and threatenings to agre to the same that thou belevest to be trew. Furthermore, thoughe there be one religione which alone is trew and al other vaine and superstitious, yet did he wel foresee (so that the matter were handeled with reason and sober modestie) that the trueth of the owne powre would at last issue out and come to lyghte. But if contention and debate in that behalfe should continuallye be used as the woorste men, be mooste obstinate and stubbournne, and in their evyll opinion mooste contrary; he perceaved that then the beste and holyest religion woulde be troden underfote and destroyed, by most vaine supersticions, even as good corne is by thornes and weedes overgrowen and chooked. Therefore all this matter he lefte undiscussed, and gave to every man free libertie and choise to beleve what he woulde." [1]

The Utopia was received by the scholars of Christendom, as the expression of enlarged views of the wisest polity, which should direct and control "the best commonwealthe." It was written in Latin, and translated into English, French, Italian, German, and Spanish.

The laws of Utopia upon the subject of religion, were the same in principle as the provisions of the Act concerning religion, subsequent to the first section.

The latter forbade "unreasonable disputations in point of religion." They prohibited any one from using reproachful words or speeches, or upon any occasion of offence, in a reproachful manner, calling or denominating any one in the Province, an Heretick, Schismatic, Idolator, Puritan, Presbyterian, Independent, Popish Priest, Jesuit, Jesuitical Priest, &c., enumerating seventeen names which might be applied by heated sectaries to different denominations.

They denounced punishments against the profanation of the "Sabaath, or Lord's Day, called Sunday."

---

[1] Utopia, Book 2, chap. "Of the Religions in Utopia," p. 115-6. Arber's reprint, London, 1869.

Among the seventeen epithets of reproach which are forbidden to be used, "Prelatists" is not enumerated. The "Sabaath, or Lord's Day," was the Puritan designation of Sunday, and "Prelatist" the Puritan term of reproach for members of the Church of England, and these particulars indicate that the compromise was proposed by a Roman Catholic authority, for acceptance by a Puritan Assembly, and thus was amended by it.

The Puritan party was dominant in England. The Roman Catholics controlled the government in Maryland, and the Jesuits exercised great influence over those Roman Catholics. Therefore Father More was the most appropriate person to prepare and propose the basis of settlement between Roman Catholics and Puritans.

On the subject of religious toleration, it is not surprising if the great-grandson of Sir Thomas More should have adopted the ideas of Utopia, and should have embodied them in the statute drawn for the purpose of securing such toleration, in precisely the line marked out in the work of his ancestor. The same general design runs through Commissions, Oaths, Code of Laws and Conditions of Plantation.

They are all framed to accomplish the common object of composing existing differences, and constitute one entire measure of compromise. This measure differs from the articles of agreement or secret treaty, in this — that it is within the powers conferred on the Proprietary, and the freemen of the Province, by the charter, and it is more comprehensive. The secret treaty could not have been made binding except by the consent of the freemen, and even then it would only have been a settlement between the Jesuits and their opponents.

The compromise was consistent with the charter. Lord Baltimore had the right to frame commissions to his officers, and thus secure religious toleration, by the weight of executive authority. He had the right to prescribe official oaths, and thus guaranty freedom of conscience by that solemn sanction. He had the right to prescribe conditions on which lands could be acquired and held, and thus enforce the Statutes of Mortmain. He had the right to propose a code of laws to be perpetual, and to give his assent to them in advance, if adopted by the freemen. He had the right to propose measures for their adoption which should secure to them the constitutional rights of Englishmen. Statesman and philosopher, he added to those rights, privileges and franchises, the necessary and logical consequence of them, yet greater than all the rest, the guaranty of liberty of conscience in matters of religion.

This course of conduct was consistent with the mature purpose of the Proprietary, as I have attempted to exhibit it, since 1633. The charter clothed him with regal prerogatives, in many respects, without check or balance. The legislative power was vested in the Proprietary and the freemen, but the former had the absolute authority to decide when, how and for what reason the latter, were to be convened. He had the power to erect Courts, to appoint judges and executive officers, to create ports and to regulate commerce.

With the executive and judicial power thus absolutely under his control, if he had followed the example set at that very time by the King of England, he would never have called an Assembly of the freemen, but would have governed by Star Chamber processes, and have levied taxes by ship money precedents, and on absolute principles. With this power in his hands, Lord Baltimore carefully prepared measures which should protect the freemen of the Province from its exercise, and constructed safeguards for their liberties, not provided in the charter.

He divested himself and his successors of the most dangerous prerogatives vested in him. His instructions to the Lieutenant General, in the Commissions of 1637, 1642 and 1644, directed him to adopt and adhere to the Common Law as the rule of right, wherever applicable to the condition of the Colony. He declined to assent to the laws passed by the General Assembly of 1635, because they did not embody his ideas of the proper policy to be pursued. He refused to agree to the adoption of the whole body of the English statutes, because many of them were inconsistent with his mature purpose.

In 1637 he sent out a code of laws by Secretary Lewger, which were first rejected because he sent them out, and then reported by a committee and passed, because the General Assembly claimed the initiative in legislation.

Of this body of laws, of which we have nothing but the titles, Bill No. 20 is "A Bill for the Liberties of the People," and No. 25 is "A Bill touching General Assemblies."

The rejected code of 1637, was substantially passed in 1638. Twenty-one of the forty-two bills of 1637 are among the thirty-six bills of 1638, and of these twenty-one bills, common to both sets of proposed laws, seventeen of them are contained in the code of 1638 which did pass and become law.

The first provision of that code is the act for establishing the House of Assembly, and the fourth section is the Act for the Liberties of the People.

Thus in 1637, in 1638, and in the Code of 1638, the distinct intent and purpose to plant and perpetuate free institutions is manifest.

The Act of 1638, for establishing the House of General Assembly, is noteworthy. The preamble declares that the freemen are entitled to all the Rights and Liberties of Englishmen, and were secured by their Charter the right to participate in making their own laws, and that therefore they provide for a General Assembly of the freemen, or their representatives, duly delegated for that purpose. The Code of 1638 contains the main guarantees of Magna Charta, and of the Petition of Right.

When, therefore, in 1648, Baltimore found the labor of his life about to be lost, and the institutions, built up with so much care for fifteen years, threatened with destruction, it would seem that Father Henry More was the most suitable person to whom he would have appealed for advice.

Unfortunately, there are no recorded facts beyond those herein set forth yet known, which prove with mathematical certainty that Father More was Baltimore's adviser in the preparation of the measures of compromise.

Circumstantial evidence only, points him out as the originator of the plan, and the counsellor who prepared and proposed the measures adopted by the Proprietary. Baltimore certainly did not prepare them. They were not prepared by his direction. They were "proposed to him," and he "finding them fit, assented to them."

They were certainly proposed by a Roman Catholic of authority, of learning, and of wisdom, who was a scholar and a statesman.

That Roman Catholic must have been fully informed as to the condition of Maryland, of its feuds political and feuds religious, of the quarrel between the Roman Catholic proprietors and priesthood, and the majority consisting of Protestants, generally of humble position. He must have agreed with Baltimore in the policy of Mortmain, and yet have been unfriendly to Lewger, the party who introduced and enforced that policy in the Province against the Jesuits. No records here nor in England, give us any clue to, or indication of, any one who fills all these requisites except Father More, and he meets every one of them. It would seem therefore very probable, if not reasonably certain, that Father Henry More, Provincial of the Society of Jesus in England, was either the author, or the inspiration of the author, of the Act concerning Religion.

It has thus been shown how Cecil Calvert, by successive efforts and assiduous labor in fifteen years, divested himself of the absolute power vested in him by the charter, and laid the foundation of Maryland solidly upon the customs and laws of ancient and free England. He secured to her people, by laws prepared by his direction, and by him propounded to the General Assembly:

1. All the provisions of Magna Charta.
2. The right to meet in General Assembly at least once in three years.
3. The right to the Common Law.
4. The right of trial by jury.
5. The right that no aids, subsidies, customs, taxes or impositions should be laid without the consent of the freemen in the General Assembly.
6. The right that Martial Law should never be proclaimed, except in time of camp or garrison, and then only in such camp or garrison.
7. The right that no war should be waged beyond the limits of the Province, for which the freemen should be bound to defray the expense, without their consent.
8. That all charges for any war in defence of the Province, should be defrayed by an equal assessment on all persons and property.
9. The right of Liberty of Conscience.

He could have given to the Province all these institutions by proclamation, of his own mere motion, but then they would have been subject to overthrow on every descent of the title, or change of government.

He wisely secured them to the people, by the joint act of the freemen and the Proprietary, making it thus certain that they never would be voluntarily surrendered or given up save by the consent of both.

The General Assembly met again on April 6, 1650, to complete the pacification of the Province by the adoption of the rest of the sixteen laws, as we have heretofore seen.

It consisted of the Upper House, of the Governor, Secretary, and Council, and of the Lower House, composed of fourteen Burgesses, of whom eleven were from the Roman Catholic county of St. Mary's, one from the Isle of Kent, and two from the Puritan settlement, at Providence, subsequently at this session, erected into the county of Anne Arundel. Of the Upper House, the Governor, William Stone, the Secretary, Thomas Hatton, Capt. John Price, Muster Master General and Capt. Robert Vaughan, Commander of Kent, were Protestants, and Thomas Green and John Pile, Roman Catholics.

Of the Lower House, James Cox, Thomas Sterman, John Hatch, George Puddington, Robert Robins, Walter Bain or Beane, William Brough and Francis Poesy, were Protestants. Capt. Robert Vaughan, a Protestant and Councillor, was also Burgess for the Isle of Kent, but he sat in the Upper House. The Upper House was therefore composed of five Protestants and two Roman Catholics; the Lower House of eight Protestants, and five Roman Catholics. The Lower House elected James Cox, the Burgess from Providence, their Speaker.[1]

After the adjournment of the Assembly, the Governor, and three members of his Council and Upper House, and eight members of the Lower House, and forty-three other Protestants, signed and issued a Declaration:

"That according to an Act of Assembly here, and several other strict injunctions and declarations by his Lordship for that purpose made and provided, we do here enjoy all fitting and convenient freedom and liberty in the exercise of our religion, under his Lordship's government and interest; and that none of us are any ways troubled or molested for or by reason thereof within his Lordship's said Province."[2]

The compromise of peace had therefore accomplished its object, and perfect religious liberty was enjoyed by all Christian people in Maryland.

While Cecil Calvert controlled the government in conjunction with his Protestant citizens, the compromise was maintained. But as soon as the Puritan party, under Cromwell's Commissioners obtained possession, one of the first

---

[1] See Bacon's Laws, 1650, 2 Bozman, 672, and 2 Scharf, 181-203, for the names of the members of this Assembly, and signers of the Protestant Declaration.

[2] Ib.

acts of the General Assembly called by them on October 20, 1654, declared:

"That such as profess Faith in God by Jesus Christ, though differing in Judgement from the Doctrine, Worship or Discipline publicly held forth, should not be restrained from, but protected in the Profession of the Faith, and Exercise of their Religion, so that they abuse not this Liberty to the Injury of others, Disturbance of the Peace, &c.; *Provided such Liberty shall not extend to Popery or Prelacy*, nor to such as under the profession of Christ, hold forth and practice Licentiousness."[1]

This was the first time in Maryland that any law was passed interfering with Liberty of Conscience.

The Proprietary, however, recovered possession of the government upon executing an agreement in England, on the 30th of November, 1657, signed by himself and Samuel Mathews, which stipulated among other things that the Act concerning Religion of 1649, should never be repealed.[2]

This compact repealed *proprio vigore* the persecuting Act of the Puritan Assembly of 1654.

Josias Fendall, appointed Governor by Lord Baltimore, assumed the position in 1658, and at once began to intrigue for an independent tenure.

---

[1] Bacon, 1654. 1 Scharf, p. 215.
[2] 1 Scharf, 227-8.

He was in thorough accord with the party which had been displaced, and acted under their inspiration. Providence, at the mouth of Severn, now Annapolis, was the headquarters of the Puritans.

On the 23d of July, 1659, he held a council there, at which these proceedings transpired:

"Upon consideration had of the disturbance of the Civill and Military part of the Government by the Quakers.

"Ordered as follows, viz:

"Whereas, it is well knowne in this Province, that there have of late bin severall Vagabonds and Idle persons, knowne by the name of Quakers, that have presumed to come into this Province, as well diswading the People from complying with the Military discipline in this time of Danger, as also from giving testimony, or being Jurors in cases depending betweene party and party, or bearing any office in the Province, to the no small disturbance of the Lawes and Civill government thereof; and that the Keeping and detayning them as Prisoners hath brought so great a charge upon this Province, the Governor and Council taking it into their consideration, have thought fitt, to appoint, and doe hereby for the prevention of the like inconveniences for the time to come, Require and command, all and every Justice of the Peace of this Province, that so soon as they shall have notice, that any of the foresaid Vagabonds or Idle persons, shall againe presume to come into this Province, they forthwith cause them to be apprehended and whipped, from Constable to Constable, out of the Province."[1]

This action was directly contrary to the act of 1649, and to the agreement made by the

---

[1] Lib. II. II., Proceedings of the Provincial Court, 1658 to Nov. 1662. The original record.

Proprietary in England. Fendall followed up this act of defiance of law, by executing a *coup d'etat*, whereby he freed himself and the Province, from all dependence on the lawful authority of Lord Baltimore.

In execution of the intrigue, and arrangement, made with the Puritan faction, he convened a General Assembly on the 28th of February, 1659 ᴼ·ˢ·, at which the Lower House insisted upon its right to sit with the Upper, and thereby dissolved the Government as theretofore established by law. On March 14, Fendall surrendered to the meeting thus constituted, all his authority as derived from Lord Baltimore, and was immediately elected Governor by the Assembly.

He thereupon issued his Proclamation "commanding all persons to own no authority but what immediately proceeds from his Majesty, or the Grand Assembly of this Province."[1]

Lord Baltimore, however, acted promptly, and Fendall was evicted from his usurped authority, and on the following December 11, 1660, Philip Calvert was sworn in as Governor, and assumed control.[2]

---

[1] Bacon, 1658. 1 Scharf, 206, for a full account of these proceedings.

[2] In Lib. H. H., Proceedings of the Provincial Court, March, 1658 to November, 1662, the last entry on fol. 372–373 is of the proceedings held by the Court, March 5, 1659. The next recorded page is of December 11, 1660, which is the following December, when Philip Calvert and his Council were sworn in. Fendall's usurpation took place March 14,

The Quakers were unmolested, and the Act of Peace again prevailed.

Cecil Calvert died on November 30, 1675, and was succeeded by his son, Charles, who retained the control of the Province until it was wrested from him by the Revolution of the Protestant Association of 1689. The life of Cecil was spent in struggles to found and maintain the institutions of liberty in Maryland. From June 20, 1632, until his death, more than forty-three years, he had passed through the most eventful epoch of English history. He saw Parliamentary institutions overthrown, and the whole power of government usurped by the King. He saw the monarchy destroyed, and all governmental functions absorbed by the Parliament. He witnessed the expulsion of the Parliament again, and liberty and law prostrate under the dominion of the sword, and then he lived to see the ancient balance of the Constitution restored, with King, Lords, and Commons re-established, after an in-

---

1659 O.S., which is nine days after the record of 1659 closes. The first order of the proceedings of December 11, 1660, is: "It is ordered that all acts and orders entered in the time of the defection of the government from his Lordship, being the fifth day of March, 1659, be null and of no force, and that the same be forthwith razed and torn from the records."

Five pages were accordingly "razed and torn from the records" as testified by the stubs of five pages still remaining. The written evidence therefore of Fendall's "defection" has been lost, for these five pages contained doubtless the record of his proceedings from March 14, 1659, up to the time when he was driven from the government he had usurped.

terregnum of nearly twenty years, and right and justice once again trampled upon, in the frenzy of a political and religious reaction. Under all these extraordinary convulsions of society, and revolutions of government, he succeeded in planting and preserving in Maryland, the rights of legislation by the freemen, of Habeas Corpus, of Trial by Jury, of Parliamentary taxation, of security against Martial Law, and of Liberty of Conscience.

While the King was collecting aids and subsidies in England, by the processes of the Star Chamber, no taxes or fees could be levied in Maryland save by the vote of the General Assembly. While the right of personal liberty was denied in England, by the Long Parliament, the writ of right protected the humblest citizen in Maryland.

While the New Model lived at free quarters in England, no soldier could be billeted on the homes of the people here. While the Churchmen were fining and whipping Roman Catholics and Puritans; while the Puritans were fining Churchmen and whipping Quakers, and denouncing death against all who refused to accept their creed, as laid down in their Ordinance of 1648, all alike, Churchmen, Roman Catholics, Puritans, Presbyterians and Quakers found safety, toleration, and protection in Maryland.

From 1634 until 1689, no man was ever molested in Maryland, on account of his religious opinions, except in the short intervals of Ingle's occupation, the sway of the Protector's Commissioners, and Fendall's brief usurpation.

The man who could have thus founded a State on such institutions, in such times, and have safely preserved them through such revolutions, is entitled to be ranked with those who have been great benefactors of mankind.[1]

The administration of Charles Calvert, third Lord Baltimore, was but an extension of the principles and policy of his father.

In 1681, the Quakers petitioned the General Assembly, to be allowed to affirm, instead of taking the usual oaths, in cases where oaths were by law required.

The Upper House consisted of the appointees of the Proprietary. On September 6, 1681, that House ordered: "Upon reading the paper delivered yesterday by William Berry and Richard Johns, this House do say:

"That if the rights and privileges of a free born Englishman, settled on him by Magna Charta, so often confirmed by subsequent Parliaments, can be preserved by yea and nay in wills and testaments, and other occurrents, the Lower House may do well to prepare such a

---

[1] Appendix K.

law, and then the Upper House will consider of it."

No relief having been given them by the Assembly, the Proprietary by proclamation in 1688, relieved them from the necessity of taking oaths in testamentary causes.

This statement of the facts, established by the records, concerning the foundation of Maryland, prove:

First. That Lord Baltimore did *not* undertake the management and development of his Province "without any special sense of responsibility to the community," and "that Religious toleration in Maryland must be *not* attributed solely the very commonplace law of self interest."

Second. That the act concerning Religion, was not the "echo" of any British order, or ordinance of the Long Parliament, securing or declaring Religious toleration, because the Puritans in England always, and on every occasion, when in power, persecuted all who differed with them in opinion, nor was it the work of the Protestant majority in the Province, because whenever they obtained control of the government, they immediately followed the example of their fellows at home in persecuting all others, as in 1645 under Ingle, in 1654 under Cromwell's Commissioners, and in 1659 under Fendall, the renegade Governor of Baltimore.

Third. That the principle of Toleration, or Liberty of Conscience was not adopted, and maintained by Cecil Calvert, because he was a Roman Catholic, or from the promptings of the Roman Catholic priesthood, or teachings of the Roman Catholic Church, but

Fourth. That Cecil Calvert, being vested with extraordinary power over a great territory, determined to found there a free English State, where all the rights and liberties of free Englishmen, which were then in great jeopardy in England, might be enjoyed and secured to the remotest posterity forever. That to do this he divested himself, and his heirs, of the princely prerogatives granted to him by his Charter; he procured to be drafted at home, and then adopted, by the freemen of Maryland, Codes of Laws, which transferred English institutions to Maryland; that by orders, Proclamations, and Conditions of Plantation, he strengthened and fortified those institutions thus transplanted, by legislation, and that believing that Magna Charta and the Petition of Right declared the right of every Englishman to liberty of person, and security of property, he was wise enough, and brave enough, to see and declare that those rights were worthless without Liberty of Conscience. He therefore adopted and declared that to be the principle on which the foundations of

Maryland should be laid, and he from the first intended to secure all those rights, privileges and franchises, not alone to Roman Catholics, nor yet alone to Englishmen, but to all Christian people of all the nations of the world. That in doing this he was supported by the whole social influence of the Roman Catholics of England, and the power of the Society of Jesus, who thereby sought to secure for members of their Church Religious Liberty, denied them in England. From the landing at St. Mary's on the 27th of March, 1634, to this day, Liberty of Conscience has been the fundamental institution of Maryland. Under it the Puritans settled at Providence, the Quakers at West River, and the Presbyterians on the Patuxent. It gave shelter to the Huguenots after the massacre of St. Bartholomew, and the Roman Catholics from the murders and the burnings of St. Domingo. The banished Arcadians found refuge here, together with the oppressed people of the Palatinate, and notwithstanding its repeated external overthrow by exterior force of faction, it has always been imbedded in the life of the people.

When the Protestant Revolution of 1689 resulted in the establishment of the Church of England, and the imposition of a Poll tax for the support of its clergy, the ancient foundation was restored by the people in 1776, as soon as they assumed the right of self government, and to this day, the Bill of Rights declares that "the levying of taxes by the Poll is grievous and oppressive" and reiterates the principle of the Act concerning Religion.

Upon the foundations thus laid by Cecil Calvert, the liberties of the people have ever since securely rested. In the long controversy between the Governor and the General Assembly, concerning the right of the former to levy taxes in the form of fees for public officers, the latter continually relied upon the unanswerable defence of the reiterated declarations of its predecessors, assented to by the Proprietaries, that no taxes, aids, or subsidies, could ever be levied, unless by the representatives of the freemen.

And to the claim of the Parliament, at a later day, of the power to tax the Province, the ancient right of Maryland, under her Charter, and under her Acts of Assembly, never to be taxed unless by her own consent, was interposed as the insurmountable protection against usurpation.

In all the wars, and insurrections, revolutions, rebellions, and civil broils, which have swept the Province, neither life, liberty, nor property have ever been sacrificed, in the fury of religious fanaticism.

Blood has been shed in the struggles of faction, but no man has ever been put to death on account of his religion.

The Jesuit Fathers acquired, in 1637, the manors of St. Inigoes, St. Thomas, St. George's Island, and Cedar Point.[1]

They there established their altars and their chapels. For two centuries and a half they have enjoyed them undisturbed, for the use of the Church, and the support of the Society, a perpetual monument of the liberal institutions on which the foundations of Maryland rest, and of the ever-pervading influence of the wise and far-seeing policy of the Founder.

These institutions, and that policy, have become fundamental in all the American commonwealths, and are being recognized and adopted as those on which alone civilization can be developed.

---

[1] Appendix L.

APPENDIX.

APPENDIX A, (p. 8.)

THE WOODSTOCK LETTERS.

"The Woodstock Letters" is a monthly periodical, printed by the Jesuits, at the Jesuit College, at Woodstock, Maryland, for private circulation among the Society of Jesus.

It is devoted to Historical and Missionary discussion and information, and contains many valuable and curious publications concerning the Society in the early history of Maryland. It is not published for general circulation.

I am indebted to Rev. Edward McGurk, S. J., President of Loyola College, for access to these papers and to the Library of the College, and to Brother O'Rourke, S. J., the Librarian, for assistance in my investigations there; to the Rev. Robert Fulton, S. J., Provincial of Maryland and President of Georgetown College, for assistance; to the authorities of Woodstock College for copies of Stonyhurst MSS., herein first given to the historical student, which have been translated for me by Father Ward, S. J. The Provincial of England, Father Purbrick, S. J., and Brother Henry Foley, S. J., editor of the Records of the English Province, have courteously given me access to original records, for which I return my thanks.

Dr. William H. Browne, Librarian of Johns Hopkins University, has translated for me the curious paper relating to the Three Propositions for Religious Toleration to the English Parliament in 1645–47, and I hereby make my acknowledgments to him for the same.

APPENDIX B, (p. 21.)

Thomas Howard, Earl of Arundel, and Thomas Arundel, Baron Arundel of Wardour.

It is probable that the Arundel who, with George Calvert, applied in February, 1630, for a grant, was the Earl of Arundel, Thomas Howard, and not the Baron Arundel of Wardour, Sir Thomas Arundel. The entry is:

"February 10, 1630.—Articles which A and B request the Attorney General to grant to them by Patent, for the settlement and plantation of Carolana, the 34 and 35 deg. of Nor. lat., 'within his Province of Carolana,' to be peopled and planted by them. Power to erect courts. Two-thirds of the Territory to be held of him in the King's service, with titles of honor, the rest in free socage."— Calendar of State Papers, Colonial, 1574–1660, p. 107.

On page 28, same volume, is the entry:

"March 27, 1622.— Grant to Sir Thomas Arundel, of the Island called the Basse, lying N. by W. from Ireland, not yet inhabited, to hold for fifty years, at a yearly rent of £5."

The Earl of Arundel was, in 1619, a member of the Council with Sir George Calvert — Calendar, 1574–1660, p. 23.

"March 16, 1621.—Pet. for grant of Newfoundland referred to Ld. Steward, Ld. Chamberlaine, Earl of Arundel, Lord Vis. Falkland and Sect'y Calvert to report."— p. 25–26.

"July 24, 1622.—The Bonds for dividends of the Duke of Lennox, the Earl of Arundel, and Sect'y Calvert agreed upon."

Neill's Colonization in America, p. 213–214, says that "the Duke of Norfolk contemplated a settlement in 1629, south of the James river, and the Virginia Assembly, in compliment to him, made a new county bearing his name." There was no Duke of Norfolk in 1629. Thomas Howard, 4th Duke, was attainted and beheaded in 1572, and the title became extinct. His grandson,

Thomas, was made Earl of Norfolk in 1644, and his grandson Duke of Norfolk in 1664.[1]

The Earldom of Arundel was one of the dignities of the family of Howard, and was inherited by Philip Howard, by right of his mother, heiress of Fitzalan, as Earl, about 1580.

Thomas Howard was the Earl of Arundel, who was concerned in the grant of Newfoundland with Calvert.

Neill says, p. 213, that two weeks after the petition of Arundel and Baltimore for a grant out of Carolana, a charter was prepared therefor and signed, but it caused so much opposition from Francis West, brother of Lord Delaware; William Clayborne, Secretary, and William Tucker, one of the Virginia company who was in London, that it was abandoned. He then persuaded the King to give him a grant embracing the more remote lands north and east of the Potomac River. In a note to page 214, he says, this southern tract must have been the same as that which the Duke of Norfolk obtained, who was the brother of his daughter-in-law, the wife of his son Cecilius.

In this Neill is mistaken. There was, as I have shown, no Duke of Norfolk, and the Earl of Arundel was a very different person from the Baron of Arundel, of Wardour, the father-in-law of Cecil Calvert. The one was the head of the house of Howard — the other of the family of Arundel. The house of Howard was the most illustrious in England. It was descended from Thomas Plantagenet, eldest son of Edward I., on the one side. It was heir to the honors and estates of Mowbray, Duke of Norfolk, and Fitzalan, Earl of Arundel. It was invested with the office of Earl Marshall in 1385.

The first Howard, Duke of Norfolk, fell on Bosworth field.

The head of the House was Duke of Norfolk, Earl of Arundel, Surrey and Norfolk, Baron Fitzalan, Clun, Oswaldestrie and Maltravers, Earl Marshal and Hereditary Marshal of England, Premier

---

[1] Burke's Peerage, Norfolk.

Duke, and Earl, immediately after the princes of the blood royal. Thomas Howard was born 1592, and died October 4, 1646.

If he was the Arundel who was the colleague of Baltimore, (and the above furnishes grounds for believing that he was) in the Catholic undertaking, for a Catholic emigration to found a Catholic refuge, then the enterprise would have been sustained by even greater influence than if Baron Arundel, of Wardour, had been the party to it. Thomas, Baron Arundel of Wardour, died, according to Burke, November 7, 1630.

The application of Baltimore and Arundel for a grant of part of Carolana, was made February 10, 1630, according to the calendar of State papers.

If this was 1630 $^{O.S.}$, the application was made after the death of the Baron, and therefore must have been made by the Earl. But the dates in the calendar are presumed to be conformed to the New Style, and therefore the application was made before Arundel of Wardour, died. In the text, I have attributed the application to him. His family was second only to that of Howard, Earl of Arundel. His grandmother was daughter of Edmund Howard, son of the third Duke of Norfolk, and sister of Catherine Howard, Queen of Henry VIII.

Either Earl Arundel, or Baron Arundel, would have represented the great Roman Catholic Peers and families of England.

APPENDIX C, (p. 32.)

Protestant Majority.

"Freeman" designated every citizen above the age of 21 and not held to personal service by indenture or otherwise. In 1642, Thomas Weston claimed to be exempt from service in the General Assembly because he had no land nor certain dwelling house then, but it was voted that he was a freeman and bound to appear, which he did and took his seat.[1]

John Robinson, carpenter, claimed his seat as a freeman, in 1637, and was admitted.[2]

So did Edward Bateman, carpenter, and Roger Oliver, mariner, and were admitted.[3] Likewise Thomas Boys, mariner, John Hill and John Nevill.

All the freemen of the Province were summoned by special writ or by public notice to appear and attend the General Assembly of 1637.

Sixty-seven were actually summoned, and on January 25, 1637, the first day of meeting, "there was proclaymed that all freemen, omitted in the writ of summons, that would clayme a voyce in this General Assembly should come and make their clayme."[4]

Eight freemen are recorded as having made their claim, which was allowed.

Only ninety freemen, however, appeared in person or by proxy. This proves that the rest of the men were indentured servants. In the following July 3, 1638, in the proceedings against William Lewis, for using opprobrious language about Protestant ministers, to Francis Gray and Robert Sedgrave, the witnesses were Gray, Sedgrave, Christopher Carnoll, Ellis Beach and Robert Duke. Gray had been a member of the General Assembly and therefore was a freeman. But Carnoll, Beach and Duke were not members, because they were servants. The term of service was generally about five years, and therefore the servants, brought over in 1634, became freemen by 1640, and the number of freemen increased every year, by expiration of term of service and by new arrivals.

The assessment on the freemen on September 13, 1641, designates one hundred and forty-six persons to be taxed, of whom

---

[1] 1 Scharf, p. 125-126.
[2] Streeter Papers, p. 19.
[3] Streeter Papers, p. 21.
[4] Streeter Papers, p. 18.

three were women. That of December, 1641, names one hundred and forty-one taxables.

The tax levied on each shows the social condition of those entitled to political power.

The assessment of September is for 806 lbs. of Tobacco on the taxables of St. Maries, and 404 lbs. on those of the Isle of Kent. In St. Maries, the amounts levied were:

Mr. Lewger,	30 lbs.	Mr. Binx,	20 lbs.
Mr. Blount,	30 "	Mr. Fenwick,	20 "
Mr. Langford,	30 "	Thos. Baldridge,	20 "
Capt. Cornwaleys,	200 "	Nath. Pope,	20 "
Mrs. Tranton,	30 "	Nicholas Cossin,	20 "
Mrs. White,	20 "	Nicholas Hug,	10 "
Mrs. Gerard,	30 "	Walter Bean,	10 "
Mr. Weston,	50 "		

Fifteen taxables pay 530 lbs.

The remaining 276 lbs. was levied on sixty-two taxables, in from 2 to 5 lbs. each. In Kent the levy was for 404 lbs.

Mr. Giles Brent,	100 lbs.	Nicholas Brown,	10 lbs.
Lieut. Vaughn,	10 "	Edmund Perry,	10 "
Mr. Luddington,	10 "	John Bennett,	10 "
Mr. Thompson,	10 "	William Cox,	10 "
John Abbott,	10 "	John Smith,	10 "
John Gresham,	10 "		

Eleven taxables pay 200 lbs.

The remaining 204 lbs. was levied on fifty-one taxables, 4 lbs. each person.[1]

So in the Colony at large, twenty-six persons represented the basis of seven hundred and thirty of taxation, and one hundred and thirteen persons the basis of four hundred and eighty of taxation.

---

[1] Council Proceedings, 1636-1657, fol. 85, &c.

In Assembly Proceedings, 1637–1658, p. 248, is a full list of all the persons who were freemen of the Province in 1642. Among them will be found many persons who at previous periods were servants.

The following is the extract:

"BY THE LIEUTENANT GENERAL.

Whereas, I have appointed to hold a General Assembly at St. Mary's, on Monday, the 5th of September next, to consult and advise of matters much importing the safety of the Colony at this present, these are therefore to give public notice thereof to all persons whom it may concern, and to require all freemen, inhabiting within the Province, to be at the said Assembly, at the time and place aforesaid, either by themselves or their deputies, or delegates sufficiently authorized, there to consult and advise touching the matters aforesaid, whereof not to fail at their peril.

Given at St. Mary's this 22d August, 1642.

A copy hereof sent to Kent by John Hollis.

FIFTH SEPTEMBER, 1642.— MORNING.

Assembled:

Governor,
Capt. Cornwaleys,
Mr. Giles Brent,
Mr. Secretary,
Mr. Surveyor General,
David Whitcliff,
George Pye,
Mr. Greene,
Mr. Clerk,
Mr. Weston,
Cyprian Thoroughgood,
Nicholas Herby,
Mr. George Binks,
John Hollis, carp.,
Jo. Weynill,
Thomas Franklin,
Thomas Hebden,
Francis Posie.

Appeared:

Nathaniel Pope,
Joseph Edlo,
John Norman,
John Halfhead,
John Cockshall.

By their Proxie, Mr. Thomas Greene.

Cuthbert Fenwick,
Jo. Holderne,
Richard Cope,
Andrew Monroe,
Robert Percy,
John Cook,
Daniel Clocker.
} By their Proxie, Capt. Thomas Cornwaleys.

Philip West,
Edward Parker.
} By their Proxie, Mr. Secretary.

Barnaby Jackson,
Thomas Murris,
Robert Dixon.
} By their Proxie, Mr. Geo. Binks.

Richard Call,
Walter Beane.
} By their Proxie, David Whitcliffe.

Robert Kedger, by his Proxie, George Pye.

Richard Banks,
William Wright.
} By their Proxie, Rand Revell.

James Johnson,
John Name.
} By their Proxie, Thomas Hebden.

Richard Garnett,
Lewis Froman.
} By their Proxie, Nicholas Hervey.

Walter Cottrell,
Francis Van Rynden,
Henry Bishop,
Walter King,
Thomas Petit,
John Gye,
Simon Demibiell.
} By their Proxie, Fra. Posie.

INHABITANTS OF KENT.

William Nauforn,
Thomas Allen,
John Bennett,
Henry Morgan,
Thomas Pett,
Thomas Stent,
Giles Basha,
Thomas Keyne,

Francis Robnett,
Murray Butler,
Walter Weeks,
Edward Comins,
John Russell,
Thomas Parker,
Thomas Hales,
William Cox,

Francis Brooks,
William Lant,
William Parry,
Robert Philpott,
Nicholas Porter,
George Crouch,
Robert Hewett,
Robert Lake,
John Pattner,
William Wielder,
Richard Thompson,
Edward Parry,
Devor Godwin,
Thomas Dier,
Robert Short,
Nich. Pothampton,
Roger Baxter,
John Smith,
Richard Puitevant,
John Abbott,
Dirck Derritz,
Philip Conner,
John Walker,
John Lee,
Walter Smith,
Henry East,
John Powell,
James Johnson,
Henry Bellamy,
Ralph Pettiman,
Thomas Kidd,
John Medcalfe,
John Gresham,
John Marwood,
William Jackson,
Richard Smith,
Richard Spain,
William Smith,
William Ashbrook,
Nicholas Browne,
John Hill,
Mathew Rodan,
Thomas Arnold,
Richard Primer,
Howell Morgan,
John Armsby,
Edward Thompson,
Thomas Bradnock,
John Philips,
Robert Vaughan,
Andrew Basha,
Richard Hoben,
Charles Steward,
John Pere,
Hughe Jones,
James Claughton,
William Porter.

All the above appeared by their proxie, Mr. Giles Brent.

Col. Francis Trafford, Esq.,
Capt. William Blount, Esq.,
Roger Oliver,
Robert Kedger,
Richard Duke,
Mr. James Neale.
} Excused for their absence, as being out of the Province, or County.

Robert Ellison,
Peter Draper,
John Harrington,
William Marshall,
John Stigg,
Arnold Fresh,
Joseph Gregory,
John Court,
Mr. Dracutt.
} Suspended from amercem't till they have notice that their presence is required, by themselves, or their Proxies.

All these following amerced 20 lbs. tobacco for not appearing by themselves or proxie upon call, till they purge their contempt:

William Hawkins,
Ellis Beach,
Robert Nicholls,
John Thatcher,
Henry Brooks,
William Tomson,
William Durford,
Jo. Hampton,
John Norton,
Thomas Orly,
Thomas Thomas,
Isaac Edwards,
Nicholas Cossin,
John Harwood,
John Elkin,
William Bretton,
Robert Tully,
John Tomson,
Simon Richardson,
Richard Hill,
Henry Hooker,
Thomas Boys,
Thomas Baldridge,
Thomas Willis,
Henry James,
Thomas Allen,

Christopher Carnoll,
Edward Cottam,
Thomas Davis,
Nicholas Keytin,
Stephen Thomas,
Mark Pheypo,
Barth. Lewis,
Peter Marril,
Robert Smith,
William Edwin,
John Warren,
John Rutlidge,
Henry Lee,
William Marfennes,
John Sutton,
John Robinson, carp.
John Langworth,
William Broughe,
John Medley,
Thomas Bushell,
Alexius Hooper,
William Hardedge,
John Hollis, carp.
Joseph Buskett,
John Prettiman,
James Cauther,

Thomas White,	Anthony Rawlins,
Thomas Sterman,	John Langford,
John Price,	William Browne,
Thomas Pewett,	John Marlburgh,
Arthur C. Hay,	Francis Pope,
Thomas Pasmore,	John Nevitt,
John Rolium, car.,	Hangat Baker,
Edward Hull,	Mr. Gerard,
William Cook,	Joseph Cordell, coop.,
Robert Edwards,	John Hatch,
Edward Sympson,	John Worthy,
John Mansell,	Richard Nevitt.

Mr. Thomas Weston being called, pleaded he was no freeman, because he had no land, nor certain dwelling here, &c., but being put to the question it was voted that he was a freeman, and as such bound to his appearing, by himself, or proxie, whereupon he took place in the house."

In the afternoon Francis Gray and Thomas Franklin, whose names do not appear in the morning's proceedings, appeared by proxie. Two hundred and sixteen freemen are named.

Sedgrave, Beach, and Carnoll, the servants of 1638, were freemen in 1642, and members of this Assembly.

It appears that none of the Jesuits were summoned, although Father White and others were then in the Province.

In the original emigration, I think by far the largest number were servants and under indenture. The claims for land grants show that each of the persons of quality had brought out many servants. Thus John Lewger arrived, November 28, 1637, with his wife and one son, and three maid servants, and three men servants, and a boy.

The "twenty gentlemen" probably averaged six servants, male and female.

The adventurers who came over in the first six years, I suppose came on the same general plan, to wit: men of property removing their fortunes with their families, of servants, mechanics and laborers. The Conditions of Plantation advise them what sort of mechanics to take out. The expiration of the terms of service had made freemen of many of the servants by 1640-41, whereby the political power and control passed to the Protestants.

Therefore, Father Henry More, in his letter to the Cardinal Prefect, in 1641-42, cited in full in the text, says that Lewger summoned an Assembly consisting almost entirely of heretics.

This was the Assembly of October 25, 1640, which passed the law touching marriages.

The Puritans from Virginia came in 1649-50, and settled at Providence, and the Protestant majority I think must constantly have increased. Baltimore invited Germans, French, Spaniards, and Italians, to come in. Very few came. The facility with which Ingle overturned the government of Leonard Calvert, proves that the population sympathized with the Parliament. The curious *coup d'etat* of Fendall, proves that the people sympathized with the Puritans, and refused to acquiesce in the delivery of the Province to Baltimore. The Protestant Associators of 1689, overthrew the government without a blow. Thus Ingle in 1644, the Puritans in the battle of Severn in 1655, Fendall's usurpation in 1659, and the Protestant Associators and John Coode in 1689, all prove to me that the Protestant majority was constantly recalcitrating against the Roman Catholic minority, who enjoyed the offices and controlled the Upper House. Minorities do not rebel four times in forty-five years, without gross oppression and cruelty.

No cruelty nor oppression ever existed under Cecil or Charles Calvert; hence, I infer that the commotions above named, were the struggles of the majority to obtain control and privileges.

The ascertained population at different periods also tends to prove this hypothesis.

1667, February 8, the Assembly sat at Patuxent.

It ordered a levy of every twentieth person to be raised for the expedition against the Indians. There were assigned to

Calvert, ...	89 men.	Charles, . . .	52 men.
St. Mary's, . .	69 "	Baltimore, .	36 "
Anne Arundel, . .	62 "	Somerset, .	25 "
Talbot, . . .	62 "	Kent, .	14 "
			409

Total population in 1667, 8,180 souls.

Chalmers, quoted by Hawks, (Md. Eccl. Contr., 59.) says: "It is indeed true that at this time, 1692, from the testimony of an eye witness, there were thirty Protestants to one Papist in the Province."—Chalmers, note 24, p. 376.

This was just after the Protestant Revolution. Dr. Bray, in a memorial to the House of Bishops in England, in 1700, says: "The Papists in this Province, Maryland, appear to me not to be above a twelfth part of the inhabitants."—Maryland Toleration, Allan, p. 56.

A census of the number of Papists was taken by the Sheriffs, in their respective counties, by order of Governor Seymour, in 1708. Total number in the Province, 2,974. Total population, 40,000.—London Public Record Office, Maryland B. T. Red. No. 4 H, p. 79, cited in the Woodstock Letters, vol. 10, p. 15.

All these facts prove the original and continued predominance of the Protestant population over the Roman Catholics.

APPENDIX D, (p. 34.)

CORNWALEYS.

I have accepted the statement of Mr. Neill, that Capt. Thomas Cornwaleys was a Protestant. I can find no proof of his religious connection, in the records.

He was the most influential and important personage in the Province, and as late as 1641 he paid one quarter of the entire taxes of St. Mary's county. (See Appendix C.) Neill, in English Colonization of America, page 251, gives the time and place of his death and the names of his descendants who were clergymen of the Church of England for a century, as below stated.

Capt. Thomas Cornwaleys was son of Sir William and grandson of Sir Charles, who was Ambassador to Spain under James I. He was son of Sir Thomas, Treasurer of Calais and Comptroller of the household of Queen Mary. The family was Protestant, but some of them became Roman Catholics.

Father Richard Cornwaleys, in 1598 entered the English College at Rome. He was then 30 years old, born a heretic, but his father, Henry Cornwaleys, had not long since become reconciled to the Roman Catholic Church. He was a fellow of Caius College, Cambridge, and second wrangler of his day.

His relatives were Sir Thomas Cornwaleys, Catholic, Sir William Cornwaleys, who married the heiress of Baron Latimer, and his brother Charles, who were not Catholics. He had a younger brother and two sisters, and two half brothers by his mother, one of whom was a priest. He was converted by Father Gerrard and took the Jesuit name of Richard Fincham, and died in the palace of the English Ambassador, in Spain.—Records English Province, S. J., vol. I, p. 181.

The English Ambassador was his brother Charles, a Protestant, and grandfather of our Capt. Thomas Cornwaleys.

The last named was appointed Councillor in 1632; commanded force against Claiborne in 1635; opposed the Code proposed by Lord Baltimore, 1638; Deputy Governor, by Leonard Calvert, 1638; appointed Lieutenant General by Leonard Calvert, during his absence, June 24, 1641; appointed to the New Council, and refuses to be sworn, 1642; commands force against Indians, and protests, in the Assembly, against the Governor and his servants being exempted from military service, August and September, 1642; commands force against Indians, 1643; Councillor again, 1644.

His manor was named Cornwaley's Cross. It was plundered by Ingle, when he took possession of St. Mary's, in February, 1645, and much valuable plate and furniture taken.

Suit was brought, in his name, in 1646, in an action of trespass, *quare clausum*, against Ingle, in London, for damage done to his house and furniture, and damages laid at £3,000. Ingle thereupon presented his petition to the House of Lords, in which he charges that "since his return to England, the said Papists and malignants conspiring together have brought fictitious actions against him at the Common Law, in the name of Thomas Cornwaleys and others, for pretended trespass." (See Neill's Colonization, page 249, for the petition in full.)

March 7, 1642, he received a grant for 4,000 acres, beyond Port Tobacco Creek. Member of the General Court, November 25, 1652. Assistant Governor to Governor Fendall, November 20, 1657. He returned to England, sailing June 2, 1659.

In September, 1663, William Calvert and Thomas Noltey, Esq's., presented to the Upper House the petition of Captain Cornwaleys, in the nature of what is now called a Bill for Relief, against a "surreptitious judgment." The House ordered a new trial before the Provincial Court, as a Court of Chancery.— Streeter Papers, 211.

He died in 1676, at Burnham Thorpe, Norfolk. His son, Rev. Thomas, was a rector in Suffolk, died 1731; his son, Rev. William, also rector in Suffolk, died 1786; his son, Rev. William, rector in Kent, died 1837; his daughter, Caroline Frances, the last of the line, authoress of "Small Books on Great Subjects," died unmarried, 1858.—Neill's Maryland not a R. C. Colony, p. 2.

LIST OF SERVANTS BROUGHT IN BY CAPT. THOMAS CORNWALEYS.

A. D. 1633-1634.

Twelve in the Ark, besides five more received by the death of his partner, John Saunders.

John Hallowes,
John Holden,
Josias—drowned.
Cuthbert Fenwick,
Christopher Martin,

Roger Walter,
Roger Morgan,
John Norton, Sr.,
John Norton, Jr.

1635.

William Penshort,
John Medley,
Richard Brock,
John Gage,
Richard Cole,

Richard Brown,
Zachary Mottershead,
Walter Walterling,
Francis Van Eyden.

1636.

John Cook,
Tho. York—killed at Nantioke.

Daniel Clocker,
Richard Hill,
Restitua Tue.

1637.

Charles Maynard,
Stephen Gray,
Francis Shirley,

Ann Wiggin,
Alice Moreman.

1639.

Nicholas Gwyther,
Edmund Jacques,
Richard Farmer,
Edmund Deering,
George, a tailor,

William Freak,
Morris Freeman,
Jeremiah Coote,
Martha Jackson.

1640.

William Durford,
Henry Burke,
George, a smith,

Edward Matthews,
Hannah Ford.

1641.

Francis Anthell,	Richard Harris,
Richard Harvey,	Thomas Harrison,
Edward Ward,	Mary Phillips,
Robert King,	John Wheatley,
Charles Rawlinson,	Wheatley's wife.

1642.

Thomas Rockwood,   Elizabeth Batte.
John Rockwood,

1646.

Magdalene Wittle.

1651.

Robert Curtis,	John Maylande,
William Sinckleare,	John Eston,
Thomas Frisell,	Sarah Lindle.
William Wells,	

Neill, Founders of Maryland, p. 77, gives this as the list of Cornwaleys' servants, for bringing in of whom he secured lands under the Conditions of Plantation.

Of them, Cuthbert Fenwick, John Norton, Christopher Martin, John Medley, and Zachary Mottershead, had become freemen and were members of the General Assembly of 1637.—Streeter papers, p. 57. Five out of twenty, brought in before 1637.

Compare this list with that of the freemen summoned to attend the General Assembly of 1642, in Appendix C, and thus see how many had become freemen at that period.

APPENDIX E, (p. 112.)

WILLIAM STONE.

The commission to William Stone bearing date August 6, 1648,[1] recites: "That whereas our trusty and well-beloved William Stone, now or late of Northampton county, Virginia,

---

[1] Council Proceedings, 1636 to 1657.   [2] Bozman, 642-649.

Esq, hath undertaken, in some short time to procure five Hundred people of British or Irish descent, to come from other places and plant and reside in our said Province of Maryland for the advancement of our Colony there."

He arrived in the Province early in 1649, and brought in six persons with him.[1]

Neill, says,[2] that the Puritan settlement of Nansemund, in Virginia, removed under Governor Stone's auspices to Providence, in Maryland. They may have been the five hundred that Stone undertook to procure to come from other places. They certainly arrived at the mouth of Severn, Providence, now Annapolis, about this time. Davis thinks that Governor Stone was from Northamptonshire, in England, because his county in Virginia and a manor in Prince George's county, Maryland, belonging to Thomas Sprigg, whom he calls brother, both bore that name.

According to tradition in the family, narrated by Hon. Frederick Stone, he was granted as much land as he could ride around in a day, and he thus surveyed and acquired his manor on Nanjemy River, in Charles county, called Avon.[3] According to the same authority he was twice married, one of his wives being a Roman Catholic.

Thomas Stone, his great-great-grandson, was member of the Continental Congress, from Maryland, and one of the signers of the Declaration of Independence.

Michael Jenifer Stone, another great-great-grandson, was member of the Convention of Maryland, which ratified the Constitution of the United States. John Hawkins Stone, another great-great-grandson, was Captain in the Maryland Line, and Governor in 1794. The Right Reverend William Murray Stone, a lineal descendant, was the third Bishop of the Protestant Episcopal Church in Maryland.

---

[1] Lib. No. 2, p. 425. Day Star, 176.
[2] English Colonization, p. 236.
[3] Lib. No. 12, p. 116. Day Star, 175.

Frederick Stone, another direct descendant in the sixth degree, has been member of Congress from Maryland, Commissioner to simplify the Pleadings at Common Law, elected by the General Assembly, and is at this time Judge of the Court of Appeals of Maryland.

He resides in Charles county, the place of his birth.

APPENDIX F, (p. 115.)
The Statutes of Mortmain.

At Common Law, any man might dispose of his lands to any other private man, at his own discretion. But it was necessary for corporations to have a license from the Crown to purchase lands in Mortmain. Lands so held were *in mortua manu*, and thus accumulated in *the dead hand*, through generation to generation, became a cause of great jealousy.

The clergy gathered great dotations of religious houses, during the first two centuries after the Norman Conquest, until a large part of the lands of the Kingdom were in the hands of corporations which never die.

The second of Henry III.'s great charters, prohibited acquisition of lands by religious *houses*.

But this statute did not prohibit acquisition by Bishops, and other corporations sole, and, as Coke says, they crept out of the statute by taking conveyances to ecclesiastical persons and not to religious houses.

The statute *de religiosis*, 7 Edward I., prohibited any person, religious or otherwise, from taking lands in Mortmain. This stopped all alienation of lands for religious or other purposes, in Mortmain. But the ingenuity of the clergy was a second time equal to the emergency and they invented the action of Common

Recovery, by which the religious houses brought fictitious suits for the recovery of land to which they had no title, and, by collusion and consent of the real owners, recovered judgment for such lands.

This was not alienation by act of the party, but was recovery by judgment of the Court.

The statute of Westminster, 13 Edward I., ch. 32, stopped this device, by enacting that on such fictitious recoveries the title should be forfeited to the lord of the fee. And the statute *quia emptores*, 18 Edward I., specially prohibited again any kind of alienation in Mortmain.

Ecclesiastical ingenuity then invented the doctrine of uses, which is, that land may be conveyed absolutely to any person for his own use or benefit, but if the conveyance be accompanied by any direction or instruction that he shall pay over the rents and profits to another, that the Court of Equity, then consisting of clergymen, would compel him to perform the trust.

The statute 15 Richard II., ch. 5, prohibits the holding to such uses.

Large tracts had also been purchased adjacent to churches and consecrated as churchyards, and this statute declared such tracts within the Statutes of Mortmain.

The last statute is 23 Henry VIII., which declares that all future grants of land for a longer term than twenty years for superstitious uses, such as obits or chanteries, shall be void.

The Conditions of Plantation only prohibits acquisition of land contrary to the Statutes of Mortmain, enacted prior to the time of Henry VIII. Therefore, it would seem that 23 Henry VIII., was not intended to be put in operation by the Conditions.

APPENDIX G, (p. 121.)

The Act Concerning Religion.

The Woodstock Letters, vol. 10, p. 1, contains papers prepared by Father George Hunter, Superior of the Maryland Mission of Jesuits in 1757. Among these papers, is a memorial to the General Assembly, protesting against a double tax on Roman Catholics, which sets forth their claim to Religious Toleration, and the proof of their right to it.

This Memorial alleges, that on planting the Colony, Cæcilius Calvert, caused declarations to be sent forth, inviting all persons, believing in Jesus Christ, to transport themselves to Maryland, . . . promising an equality of freedom and favor, and liberty of conscience to all, and further engaged to ratify his said promises by *a perpetual law.*

It further alleges, that a Law for Religious Liberty to Christians was enacted in 1640, *vide* L. 1, p. 51, and re-enacted in 1650, L. 2, p. 17, and confirmed 1656, L. 2, p. 17.

There is no record yet found containing such declaration and promise of Lord Baltimore. The Records referred to by Father Hunter, are, I fear, no longer in existence.

He is in error in referring to a law for Religious Toleration passed in 1640, led into it by the confusion produced by copying the various records.

Our original records, Libers A, B, F and Z, date back to 1636, and consist of folio volumes, the ink as fresh as if written to-day, but the corners of the leaves broken and decayed.

These Record Books begin with the signature of Leonard Calvert, in autograph, and contain proceedings of the Governor, Council, of the Provincial Court, of the Court for Causes Testamentary and Matrimonial, of Land Entries, claims and grants, of the writs to General Assemblies, of the proceedings of General

Assemblies, and of the acts passed into Laws, Proclamations, Commissions, Official Oaths, &c.

All these transactions are recorded by John Lewger, William Bretten, and Thomas Hatton, Secretaries, and their successors for some years. From these books of original entries, copies were made of the Laws into Liber W. H., which is lost, but a copy of it was made and certified by "Will Calvert" under the lesser seal at arms of the Proprietary, being the Calvert arms alone, with the leopard supporters. This seal is in red wax, and now, March, 1883, legible and in fair preservation. This is the first copy of the original records of the statutes as yet found. It must have been made prior to 1680. It includes acts from 1640 to 1678. It is the oldest *copy* we have. Liber L. L. is a copy of the Acts of 1692, made in 1695 from the original in the possession of the Commissioners of Plantation, at Whitehall, in London.

The error of Father Hunter was caused in this way. The laws were collected from the various proceedings of Assembly and copied into one book, Liber W. H.

This was again copied into Liber W. H. and L. and again into Liber C. and W. H. The original W. H. contained the Act concerning Religion as the first act in the book, which begins with the session of 1640. Hence the error was perpetuated in all the copies. But Liber W. H. and L. and Liber C. and W. H., show the mistake on the face of the record. Among the acts stated by them to have been passed at the session of 1640, is the act of amnesty for Ingle's Rebellion, between February 1645 and August 1646.

I have not been able to find any of the records referred to by Father Hunter as Libers 1 and 2, for the folios referred to by him do not correspond with W. H. and L or C. and W. H., nor with any volumes in our knowledge. The question is settled by the original record of the Council and Legislature proceedings and laws passed from May, 1649 to February, 1650 $^{o.\,s.}$, which is Old Liber A.

On folio 245, is the original autograph receipt of Thomas Hatton, Secretary, who certifies that, on the 2d day of April, 1649, he received the book, as Secretary, before the Governor and

Council. The receipt is dated April 6, 1649. On folio 268, begins the record of the Acts of Assembly of 1649, in the handwriting of Hatton.

The first Act recorded as passed, is the Act Concerning Religion, passed April 21, 1649. On the margin, in the handwriting of Philip Calvert, is this entry:

"Confirmed by the Lord Proprietor, by an instrument under his hand and seal, the 26th day of August, 1650.
PHILIP CALVERT."

In 1724–25–26 fair copies of the entire records were attempted with great care. They are sworn to be true copies by the copyist who made them and by the person who compared them, and certified to by the Council, Daniel Dulany, Sr., Thomas Bordley, John Beale, and others.

They are handsomely bound in parchment and lettered Libers 1, 2, and 3.

They are not, however, full copies, many entries in the originals being omitted.

Father Hunter is likewise in error in stating that the Act was confirmed in 1650, by an Act of Assembly. No such Act passed, but it was assented to by the Próprietary in 1650. He is likewise wrong that it was re-enacted in 1656. The Government was then under the control of Cromwell's Commissioners, and the second Act of their Assembly in 1654 was to declare Religious Liberty to all, but specially exempting from the benefits of the Act all Papists and Prelatists.

The Act of 1649 is as follows:

AN ACT CONCERNING RELIGION.

"Confirmed by the Lord Proprietor by an instrument under his hand and seal, the 26th day of August, 1650.
Philip Calvert."

"Forasmuch as in a well-governed and Christian commonwealth, matters concerning religion and the honour of our God ought in the first place to bee taken into serious consideration, and indevoured to bee settled, Bee it therefore ordayned and enacted by the right honourable Cecilius lord baron of Baltimore, absolute lord and proprietary of this province, with the advice and consent of the upper and lower house of this general assembly, that whatsoever person or persons within this province and the islands thereunto belonging, shall from henceforth blaspheme God, that is, to curse him, or shall deny our Savior Jesus Christ to be the Son of God, or shall deny the Holy Trinity, the Father, Son, and Holy Ghost, or the Godheaad or any of the sayd Three Persons of the Trinity, or the Unity of the Godhead, or shall use or utter any reproachful speeches, words or language concerning the Holy Trinity, or any of the sayd three persons thereof, shall be punished with death, and confiscation or forfeiture of all his or her land and goods to the lord proprietary and his heires.

"And bee it also enacted by the authority and with the advice and assent aforesaid, That whatsoever person or persons shall from henceforth use or utter any reproachful words or speeches concerning the blessed Virgin Mary, the mother of our Saviour, or the Holy Apostles or Evangelists, or any of them, shall in such case for the first offence forfeit to the sayd lord proprietary and his heires, lords and proprietaries of this province, the sum of 5£. sterling, or the value thereof, to bee levied on the goods and chattels of every such person so offending; but in case such offender or offenders shall not then have goods and chattels sufficient for the satisfying of such forfeiture, or that the same be not otherwise speedily satisfied, that then such offender or offenders shall be publickly whipt, and be imprisoned during the pleasure of the lord proprietary or the lieutenant or the chiefe governour of this province for the time being; and that every such offender or offenders for every second offence shall forfeit 10£. sterling, or the value thereof to be levied as aforesayd, or in any case such offender or offenders shall not then have goods or chattels within this province sufficient for that purpose, then to be publickly and severely whipt and imprissoned as is before expressed; and that every person or persons before mentioned offending herein the third time shall for such third offence forfeit all his lands and goods and be forever banisht and expelled out of this province.

"And be it also further enacted by the same Authority, advice and assent, that whatsoever person or persons shall from henceforth upon any occasion of offence or otherwise in a reproachfull manner or way, declare, call or denominate any person or persons, whatsoever inhabiting, residing, trafficking, trading or commercing, within this province, or within any the ports, harbour, creeks, or havens, to the same belonging, an Heretick, Schismatic, Idolator, Puritan, Presbyterean, Independant, Popish Priest,

Jesuit, Jesuited Papist, Lutheran, Calvinist, **Anabaptist,** Brownist, Antinomian, Barrowist, Roundhead, Separatist, or other name or terme in a reproachful manner, relating to a matter of religion, shall for every such offence forfeit and lose the sum of 10.£. sterling, or the value thereof to be levied on the goods and chattels of every such offender or offenders, the one halfe thereof to be forfeited and paid unto the person or persons of whom such reproachful words are or shall be spoken or uttered, and the other halfe to the lord proprietary and his heirs, lords and proprietaries of this province; but if such person or persons, who shall at any time utter or speak any such reproachful words or language, shall not have goods or chattels sufficient or overt within this province to be taken to satisfy the penalty aforesayd, or that the same bee not otherwise speedily satisfied, that then the person or persons so offending shall be publickly whipt and shall suffer imprisonment without bayle or mainprize until he, she, or they shall respectfully satisfie the party offended or grieved by such reproachful language, by asking him or her respectively forgiveness publickly for such his offence before the magistrate or chiefe officer or officers of the towne or place where such offence shall be given.

"And be it further likewise enacted by the authority and consent aforesayd, that every person or persons, within this province, that shall at any time hereafter prophane the Sabaath or Lord's day called Sunday, by frequent swearing, drunkenesse, or by any unciville or disorderly recreation, or by working on that day when absolute necessity doth not require, shall for every first offence forfeit 2s. 6d. sterling or the value thereof; and for the second offence 5s. sterling or the value thereof; and for the third offence and for every time he shall offend in like manner afterwards 10s. sterling or the value thereof; and in case such offender or offenders shall not have sufficient goods or chattells within this province to satisfie any of the aforesayd penalties respectively hereby imposed for prophaning the Sabaath or Lord's day called Sunday as aforesayd, then in every such case the party so offending shall for the first and second offence in that kind be imprisoned till hee or she shall publickly in open court, before the chief commander, Judge or magistrate of that county, towne or precinct wherein such offence shall be committed, acknowledge the scandall and offence hee hath in that respect given against God, and the good and civil government of this province; and for the third offence and for every time after shall also be publickly whipt.

"And whereas the inforcing of the conscience in matters of religion hath frequently fallen out to bee of dangerous consequence in those commonwealths where it hath beene practised, and for the more quiet and peaceable government of this province, and the better to preserve mutuall love and unity amongst the inhabitants here, Bee it therefore also by the lord proprietary with the advice and assent of this assembly ordained and enacted, except as in this present act is before declared and set forth, that no person or persons whatsoever within this province or the islands, ports, harbours, creeks or havens thereunto belonging, professing to believe in Jesus Christ, shall from henceforth be any waies troubled, molested, or discountenanced, for or in his or her religion, nor in the free exercise thereof within this province or the islands thereunto belonging, nor any way compelled to beleefe or exercise of any other religion against his or her consent, so as they be not unfaithful unto the lord proprietary, or molest or conspire against the civil government, established or to be established in this province under him and his heyres; and that all and every person or persons that shall presume contrary to this act and the true intent and meaning thereof, directly or indirectly, eyther in person or estate, wilfully to wrong, disturb, or trouble, or molest any person or persons whatsoever within this province, professing to believe in Jesus Christ, for or in respect of his or her religion, or the free exercise thereof within this province, otherwise than is provided for in this act, that such person or persons so offending shall be compelled to pay treble damages to the party so wronged or molested, and for every such offence shall also forfeit 20s. sterling in money or the value thereof for the use of the lord proprietary and his heires, lords and proprietaries of this province, and the other halfe thereof for the use of the partie so wronged or molested as aforesayd; or if the party so offending as aforesaid, shall refuse or bee unable to recompence the party so wronged or to satisfie such fine or forfeiture, then such offender shall be severely punished by publick whipping and imprisonment during the pleasure of the lord proprietary or his lieutenant or the chiefe governour of this province for the time being, without bail or mainprize.

"And be it further also enacted by the authority and consent aforesayd, that the sheriffe or other officer or officers from time to time to be appointed and authorized for that purpose of the county, town, or precinct where every particular offence, in this present act contained, shall happen at any time to be committed and whereupon there is heereby a forfeiture, fine, or penalty imposed, shall from time to time distrain, and seise the goods and estate of every such person so offending as aforesayd against this present act or any part thereof and sell the same or any part thereof for the full satisfaction of such forfeiture, fine, or penalty as aforesaid, restoring to the party so offending the remainder or overplus of the sayd goods and estate after such satisfaction so made as aforesayd."

The foregoing Act is recorded in Liber C. and W. H., p. 106, Liber W. H., p. 111, and Liber W. H. and L., p. 1, in the book entitled " Assembly Proceedings from 1637 to 1658," p. 354, all of which are in the Maryland Historical Society archives, except Liber W. H., which has not been found.

APPENDIX II, (p. 131.)

ORDINANCE FOR PUNISHING BLASPHEMY, &c.

This Ordinance has escaped the attention of commentators generally, because no Statutes of the Long Parliament are published in the Statutes at large after November, 1640.

It is found in "A Collection of Acts and Ordinances of General Use, made in the Parliament, November 3, 1640, until the adjournment of Parliament begun, September 17, 1656, by Henry Scobell, Clerk of the Parliament. Printed by special order of the Parliament, London, 1658."

Scobell was Clerk of the House of Commons when it was dissolved in 1653. He entered on the Journal of the House, " This day his Excellence the Lord G. Cromwell dissolved this House."

In January, 1659, when preparations were being made for the Restoration of Charles II., he was called before the bar of the House to explain how that entry came to be there, " which words the Parliament voted a forgery," says Pepys, " and demanded of him how they came to be entered. He said that they were his own handwriting, and that he did it by right of his office and the practice of his predecessors; and that the intent of the practice was to let posterity know how such and such a Parliament was dissolved, whether by command of the King, or by their own neglect, as the last House of Lords was, and that to this end he had said and writ, that it was dissolved by his Excellence the Lord G.; and that for the word 'dissolved,' he never, at the time, did hear of any other term, and desired pardon if he would not to dare *make a word himself*, but it was six years after, before they came themselves to call it an interruption."

CAP. 114.—FOR PUNISHING BLASPHEMIES AND HERESIES. FOR THE PREVENTING OF THE GROWTH AND SPREADING OF HERESIES AND BLASPHEMY.

Be it Ordained by the Lords and Commons in this present Parliament assembled. That all such persons as shall from and after the date of this present Ordinance, willingly by Preaching, Teaching, Printing or Writing, maintain and publish, that there is no God, or that God is not present in all places, doth not know and foreknow all things, or that he is not Almighty, that he is not perfectly Holy, or that he is not Eternal, or that the Father is not God, the Son is not God, or that the Holy Ghost is not God, or that they Three are not one Eternal God; Or that shall in like manner maintain and publish, that Christ is not God equal with the Father, or, shall deny the manhood of Christ, or that the Godhead and manhood of Christ are several Natures, or that the Humanity of Christ is pure and unspotted of all sin; or that shall maintain and publish, as aforesaid, That Christ did not Die, nor rise from the Dead, nor is ascended into Heaven bodily, or that shall deny his death is meritorious in the behalf of Believers; or that shall maintain and publish as aforesaid, That Jesus Christ is not the Son of God, or that the Holy Scripture (viz.) of the Old Testament, Genesis, Exodus, Leviticus, Numbers, Deuteronomy, Joshua, Judges, Ruth, 1 Samuel, 2 Samuel, 1 Kings, 2 Kings, 1 Chronicles, 2 Chronicles, Ezra, Nehemiah, Ester, Job, Psalms, Proverbs, Ecclesiastes, The Songs of Songs, Isaiah, Jeremiah, Lamentations, Ezekiel, Daniel, Hosea, Joel, Amos, Obediah, Jonah, Micah, Nahum, Habakkuk, Zephaniah, Haggai, Zacharia, Malachi; Of the New Testament, The Gospels according to Matthew, Mark, Luke, John, The Acts of the Apostles, Paul's Epistles to the Romans, Corinthians the first, Corinthians the second, Galatians, Ephesians, Philippians, Colossians, Thessalonians the first, Thessalonians the second, to Timothy the first, to Timothy the second, to Titus, to Philemon, the Epistle to the Hebrews, the Epistle of

James, the first and second Epistles of Peter, the first second and third Epistles of John, the Epistle of Jude, the Revelation of John, is not the Word of God, or that the bodies of men shall not rise again after they are dead, or that there is no day of Judgment after death; all such maintaining and publishing of such error or errors with obstinacy therein, shall by virtue hereof be adjudged Felony, and all such persons upon complaint and proof made of the same in any of the cases aforesaid, before any two of the next Justices of the Peace for that place or county, by the Oaths of two Witnesses (which said Justices of Peace in such cases shall hereby have power to administer) or confession of the party, the said party so accused shall be by the said Justices of the Peace committed to prison without Bail or Mainprise until the next Goal delivery to be holden for that place or county, and the Witnesses likewise shall be bound over by the said Justices unto the said Goal delivery to give in their evidence; And at the said Goal delivery the party shall be indicted for Felonious Publishing and maintaining such error, and in case the Indictment be found, and the Party upon his Trial shall not abjure his said error and defence and maintenance of the same, he shall suffer the pains of death, as in case of Felony without benefit of Clergy. But in case he shall recant or renounce and abjure his said error or errors, and the maintenance and publishing of the same, he shall nevertheless remain in prison until he shall finde two sureties being Subsidy men, that shall be bound with him before two or more Justices of the Peace or Goal delivery, that he shall not thenceforth publish or maintain as aforesaid the said errour or errours any more; And the said Justices shall have power hereby to take Bayl in such cases.

And be it further Ordained, That in case any person formerly indicted for publishing and maintaining of such erroneous Opinion or Opinions as aforesaid, and renouncing and abjuring the same, shall nevertheless again publish and maintain his said former errour or errours, as aforesaid, and the same proved as aforesaid, the said party so offending shall be committed to prison as formerly, and at the next Goal Delivery shall be indicted as aforesaid. And in case the Indictment be then found upon the Trial, and it shall appear that formerly the party was convicted of the same errour, and publishing and maintaining thereof, and renounced and abjured the same, the Offender shall suffer death as in case of Felony, without benefit of Clergy.

Be it further Ordained by the Authority aforesaid. That all and every person or persons that shall publish or maintain as aforesaid any of the several errours hereafter ensuing, viz. That all men shall be saved, or that man by nature hath free will to turn to God, or that God may be worshipped in or by Pictures or Images, or that the soul of any man after death goeth neither to Heaven or Hell, but to Purgatory, or that the soul of man dieth or sleepeth when the body is dead, or that Revelations or the workings of the Spirit are a rule of Faith or Christian Life, though diverse from or contrary to the written word of God; or that man is bound to believe no more than by his reason he can comprehend; or that the Moral Law of God contained in the ten commandments is no rule of Christian life; or that a believer need not repent and pray for pardon of sins; or that the two Sacraments of Baptism and the Lord's Supper are not ordinances commanded by the Word of God, or that the baptizing of infants is unlawfull, or such Baptism is void, and that such persons ought to be baptized again, and in pursuance thereof shall baptize any person formerly baptized; or that the observation of the Lord's day as it is enjoyned by the Ordinances and Laws of this Realm, is not according, or is contrary to the word of God, or that it is not lawful to joyn in publique prayer or family prayer, or to teach children to pray, or that the churches of England are no true churches, nor their Ministers and Ordinances, true Ministers and Ordinances, or that the Church Government by Presbytery is antichristian or unlawful, or that Magistracy, or the power of the Civil Magistrate, by law established in England, is unlawful, or that all use of arms, though for the publique defence (and be the cause never so just) is unlawful, and in case the Party accused of such publishing and maintaining of any of the said errors shall be thereof convicted to have published and maintained the same as aforesaid, by the testimony of two or more witnesses upon oath or confession of the said party before two of the next Justices of the Peace for the said place or county, whereof one to be of the quorum (who are hereby required and authorized to send for witnesses and examine upon oath, in such cases, in the presence of the party). The party so convicted, shall be ordered by the said Justices to renounce his said errors in the publique congregation of the same Parish from whence the complaint doth come, or where the offence was committed, and in case he refuseth or neglecteth to perform the same, at or upon the day, time, and place appointed by the said Justices, then he shall be committed to prison by the said Justices until he shall finde two sufficient sureties before two Justices of the Peace for the said place or County (whereof one shall be of the quorum) that he shall not publish or maintain the said error or errors any more.

Provided always, and be it Ordained by the Authority aforesaid, that no attainder by virtue hereof shall extend either to the forfeiture of the estate real or personal of such person attainted, or corruption of such person's blood.

2 *May*, 1648.

See Scobell's Collection, p. 149.

APPENDIX J, (p. 131,)

Ordinance against Atheistical, Blasphemous and Execrable Opinions.

Cap. 22.—Punishment of Atheistical, Blasphemous and Execrable Opinions.

The Parliament holding it to be their duty, by all good ways and means to propagate the Gospel in this Commonwealth, to advance Religion in all Sincerity, Godliness and Honesty, Have made several Ordinances and Laws for the good and furtherance of Reformation, in Doctrine and Manners, and in order to the suppressing of Prophaneness, Wickedness, Superstition and Formality, that God may be truly glorified, and all might in well doing be encouraged.

But notwithstanding this their care, finding to their great grief and astonishment, that there are divers men and women who have lately discovered themselves to be the most monstrous in their Opinions, and loose in all wicked and abominable Practises hereafter mentioned, not onely to the notorious corrupting and disordering, but even to the dissolution of all Humane Society, who rejecting the use of any Gospel Ordinances, do deny the necessity of Civil and Moral Righteousness among men; The Parliament therefore, according to the published Declaration of the Twenty Seventh of September, One thousand six hundred forty nine, To be most ready to testify their displeasure and abhorrency of such Offenders, by a strict and effectual proceeding against them, who should abuse and turn into Licentiousness, the liberty given in matters of Conscience. Do therefore Enact and Ordain, and be it Enacted and Ordained by the Authority of this present Parliament, That all and every person and persons (not distempered with sickness or distracted in brain) who shall presume avowedly in words to profess, or shall by writing proceed to affirm and maintain him or herself, or any other meer Creature, to be very God, or to be Infinite or Almighty, or in Honor, Excellancy, Majesty and Power to be equal, and the same with the true God, or that the true God or the Eternal Majesty dwells in the Creature and nowhere else; or whosoever shall deny the Holiness and Righteousness of God, or shall presume as aforesaid to profess, That Unrighteousness in persons or the acts of Uncleanness, Prophane Swearing, Drunkenness, and the like Filthiness and Brutishness are not unholy and forbidden in the Word of God, or that these acts in any person, or the persons for committing them are approved of by God, or that such acts, or such persons in those things are like unto God: Or whosoever shall presume as aforesaid to profess, That these acts of Denying and Blaspheming God, or the Holiness or Righteousness of God; or the acts of cursing God, or of Swearing prophanely or falsely by the Name of God, or the acts of Lying, Stealing, Cousening and Defrauding others, or the acts of Murther, Adultery, Incest, Fornication, Uncleanness, Sodomy, Drunkenness, filthy and lascivious Speaking are not things in themselves shameful, wicked, sinful, impious, abominable, and detestable in any person, or to be practised or done by any person or persons: Or shall as aforesaid profess, That the acts of Adultery, Drunkenness, Swearing and the like open wickedness, are in their own nature as Holy and Righteous as the Duties of Prayer, Preaching or Giving of Thanks to God: Or whosoever shall avowedly as aforesaid profess,

That whatsoever is acted by them (whether Whoredom, Adultery, Drunkenness or the like open Wickedness) may be committed without sin; or that such acts are acted by the true God or by the Majesty of God, or the Eternity that is in them; That Heaven and all happiness consists in the acting of those things which are Sin and Wickedness; or that such men or women are most perfect, or like to God or Eternity, which do commit the greatest Sins with least remorse or sense; or that there is no such thing really and truly as Unrighteousness, Unholiness or Sin but as a man or woman judgeth thereof; or that there is neither Heaven nor Hell, neither Salvation nor Damnation, or that these are one and the same things, and that there is not any distinction or difference truly between them; all and every person or persons so avowedly professing, maintaining or publishing as aforesaid, the aforesaid Astheistical, Blasphemous or Execrable Opinions or any of them, upon complaint and proof made of the same in any the cases aforesaid, before any one or more Justice or Justices of the Peace, Major or other Head-Officers of any City or Town Corporate, by the Oath of two or more Witnesses (which Oath the said Justice or Justices and Head Officer have hereby power to administer in all the cases aforesaid) or Confession of the said persons, the party so convicted or confessing, shall be by the said Justice or Justices, or other Head-Officer committed to Prison or to the House of Correction, for the space of six moneths, without Bail or Mainprize, and until he or she shall have put in sufficient Sureties to be of good behavior for the space of one whole year. And if any person or persons so convicted as aforesaid, shall at any time afterwards avowedly profess, maintain or publish as aforesaid, any of the aforesaid Atheistical, Blasphemous or Execrable Opinions, upon complaint and proof made of the same before any one or more Justice or Justices of the Peace, Major or other Head-Officer of any City or Town Corporate, by the Oath of two or more Witnesses (which Oath the said Justice or Justices, or Head-Officer have hereby power to administer) or confession of the said person, the party so confessing, or against whom proof shall be made as aforesaid, shall be by such Justice or Head-Officer sent to the Common Goal of such County, there to remain without Bail or Mainprize, until the next Assizes or Gaol-Delivery to be held for the said County; And if any such person shall be there convicted, by confession or otherwise, for such aforesaid avowedly professing, maintaining or publishing as aforesaid, any of the Atheistical, Blasphemous or Execrable Opinions aforesaid, That then the Judge or Judges before whom such Conviction shall be had as aforesaid, shall have power, and is hereby required to pronounce Sentence of Banishment upon such person so convicted as aforesaid out of the Commonwealth of England, and all the Dominions thereof: And thereupon every such person or persons so convicted and adjudged as aforesaid, shall depart out of this Commonwealth at such Haven or Port, and within such time as shall be in that behalf assigned and appointed by the said Judge or Justices, unless the same offender be letted or stayed by such reasonable means or causes as by the Common Laws of this Nation are allowed and permitted in cases of Abjuration for Felony: and in case of such let or stay, then to depart within such reasonable and convenient time after as the Common Law requireth, as in case of Abjuration for Felony as aforesaid: And if any such offender so convicted and adjudged as aforesaid, shall not go to such Haven, and within such time as is before appointed, and from thence depart out of this Commonwealth, according to this present Act; or after such his departure shall return or come again into this Commonwealth or any the Dominions thereof, without special License of the Parliament in that behalf first had and obtained, That then in every such case the person so offending, shall be adjudged a Felon, and shall suffer as in case of Felony, without benefit of Clergy. *

And to the end this Law may be the more effectually put into execution, and the growth of the aforesaid, and the like abominable and corrupt Opinions and Practises, tending to the Dishonor of God, the Scandal of Christian Religion, and the Proffessors thereof, and destructive to Humane Society, may be prevented and suppressed, Be it Enacted by the authority aforesaid, That all and every Justice and Justices of Assize, Justices of Oyer and Terminer, Justices of the Peace and Gaol-Delivery, be required and enjoyned at their Assizes and Sessions of the Peace in every County, City and Town Corporate respectively, which shall be held next after the publishing of this Act, to cause the same to be openly read and published, and do from time to time give in charge to the Grand Jury, to enquire of and present the Offences and Neglects aforesaid; which the said Justices of Assize, Justices of Oyer and Terminer, Justices of the Peace and Gaol-Delivery, have likewise by virtue of this Act, power and authority to Hear and Determine.

And be it lastly Enacted by authority aforesaid, that the Sheriffs of every County, the Majors, Bayliffs or other Head-Officers of all and every City, Borough or Town Corporate, be enjoined and required within one week after this Act shall be sent unto them or any of them, to Read, or cause the same to be Read and Proclaimed in every City, Borough or Town Corporate, upon the Market-day, and to cause the same to be affixed and set up in the publique places of such City, Borough or Town as is usual and accustomed.

Provided always, That no person or persons shall be punished, impeached, molested or troubled for any offence mentioned in this Act, unless he or she be for the same offence accused, presented, indicted or convicted within six months after such offence committed.

Passed 9 August, 1650.

See Scobell's Collection, p. 124 of the second part.

APPENDIX K, (p. 156.)

Errors of Lodge and Doyle.

Lodge and Doyle, the latest writers on the early history of Maryland, each make erroneous statements. Lodge, p. 95, says:

"The government set up (by the Charter) was a copy of the English form, or rather of the form of English government, as it ought to have been, in the opinion of George Calvert. An Assembly of Burgesses filled the place of the Parliament, and the Lord Proprietary that of the King. The constitution was exactly such a one as a high prerogative courtier in the reign of James would be likely to draw if left to himself. The Lord Proprietary was to have the right to make laws, not repugnant to those of England, when the freeholders and Burgesses could not be brought together, and he was further to have the power of granting titles and erecting Manors and Courts Baron."

Section 7 of the Charter grants to the Proprietary

"full, free and absolute power by the tenor of these presents to Ordain, Make, and Enact LAWS of what kind soever . . . of and with the *Advice, Assent and Approbation* of the FREEMEN *of the same Province, or of the greater part of them, or of their Delegates or Deputies whom* WE *will shall be called together, when and as often as need shall require, by the aforesaid now Baron of Baltimore and his heirs.*"

Section 8, grants the power to

"Make and Constitute fit and wholesome ORDINANCES from time to time to be kept and observed within the Province aforesaid, as well for the Conservation of the Peace, as for the better government of the People inhabiting therein . . . so that said ORDINANCES be consonant to reason and be not repugnant nor contrary but (so far as conveniently may be done) agreeable to the Statutes or Rights of our Kingdom of England, and so that the same ORDINANCES do not in any sort extend to oblige, bind, charge or take away the Right or Interest of any Person or Persons of or in Members, Life, Freehold, Goods or Chattels."

See the Charter in Bacon's Laws, 2 Bozman, p. 12.

Section 7 of the Charter provides for the first representative Assembly ever created under any charter, or grant of colonization.

The laws are to be made by the "advice, assent and approbation" of the *freemen*, not *freeholders*. Freemen were all who were not indentured, or apprentices, or owing service.

The power to make ordinances, granted in the next section, was to issue proclamations for police regulation, which were not to "oblige, bind, charge, or take away, the right of any person to Members, Life, Freehold, Goods or Chattels." There is no high prerogative doctrine here, but the most careful security for the liberties of the people, who are secured in the right of participation in legislation.

Doyle, p. 297, speaking of the Code sent out by the Proprietary, and rejected by the General Assembly in 1638-39, and of the bills passed by the same Assembly, in one statute, says:

"Clergy were to be exempt from capital punishment and were to be pardoned in the case of certain offences committed for the first time.

"An Act was also passed re-enacting the Statute of Edward VI., which enforced the eating of fish on certain days. That Statute had been passed by a Protestant legislature in the interests of Commerce and possibly of public health and economy. The Romanists of Maryland re-enacted it in behalf of the usage of their own Church."

No Act was passed adopting the statute of Edward VI., nor exempting the clergy from capital, or any other punishment. At least our records show none, and we have copies of all Acts passed at this session.

Again, on p. 299, he says:

"We have already seen that the Lordship of a manor carried with it a seat in the Assembly. It also gave the right of being tried by a Jury taken from among the lords of manors although with the necessary proviso, that if twelve such could not be found, their places should be supplied by freemen.

"Moreover the lords of manors were to enjoy another privilege of the English nobility, in being beheaded, if found guilty of felony, instead of being hanged."

The Lordship of a Manor carried with it no such right. All the freemen were summoned to the first Assembly of 1637-38, as our records show. All were summoned to elect Burgesses to the next Assembly of 1638-39, and the first Act they passed was to secure to every freeman the right to vote for his representatives in the Assembly.

The Upper House, by the same law, was to consist of persons summoned by special writ, and persons were summoned *not* Lords of Manors.

By the great Ordinance of 1638-39, all were to be tried by a jury, and there is no distinction between Lords of Manors, freemen, or others. No law ever secured to lords the privilege of being beheaded.

Among the bills read twice, and engrossed to be read a third time, but never read nor passed the House,[1] is "An Act for Erecting a Pretoriall."

It provides that the Lord of a Manor, for a capital offence, shall be tried by a jury of twelve Lords of Manors, if there be that many in the county, if not, then of as many Lords as there be and of freeholders, and conviction shall be by the Lieutenant General and the major part of them.[2]

But no such bill ever passed the Assembly or became a law.

Again, on pp. 304-305, he considers the Code sent out by the Proprietary in 1649, and in part adopted, at the session of 1649, by the Assembly, and then refers to the letter written by the Assembly to his Lordship, setting forth their reasons why they had refused their assent to them in full.

---

[1] Assembly Proceedings, 1637-1658, p. 55.
[2] Assembly Proceedings, 1637-1658, p. 71.

"There is," says the author, "nothing to show in what spirit Baltimore received this remonstrance."

On the contrary, Baltimore wrote a full and able reply to this letter, which is in our records, with the letter itself.—Assembly Proceedings, 1637 to 1658, p. 339 to 351. And is printed in full in 2 Bozman, 669.

In that letter he shows that the laws he sent out provide for "freedom of conscience, freedom of taxes (but such as shall be laid with the Assemblies' assent), for freedom from martial law, freedom from war contributions, and freedom of trade with the Indians." And his letter was so satisfactory that the Assembly of 1650, composed of Puritans, with a Puritan Speaker, passed every one of the laws, as he requested, which had not been assented to at the session of 1649.

Doyle, throughout, treats Baltimore as a trimmer, without conscience, seeking, at the expense of honor and conviction, to save his property rights.

The record proves that he was a statesman, intent upon forming a free commonwealth upon free English institutions, and that he took advantage of existing facts to accomplish his purpose. The surrounding circumstances altered and shifted, but through them all, he was steadfast and determined to accomplish his aim and object.

APPENDIX L, (p. 160.)

Copley's Land Grants.

Thomas Copley, Esq., made his demand for lands under the Conditions of Plantation of 1636, for transporting Mr. Andrew White, Mr. John Altham and thirty others, in 1633, and Mr. John Knowles and nineteen others, in 1637.—Kilty's Landholder's Asst., 68.

He obtained 28,500 acres, distributed the greater part to others, and retained 8,000 acres for the Society of Jesus and the use of the Church. The first tract he took up for the Society was 2,000 acres, called St. Inigoes, 1,000 acres called St. George's Island, and 400 acres of town land, about the town of St. Mary's. The second tract taken up by him, was St. Thomas and Cedar Point Neck (in Charles county, near Port Tobacco). Copley was a Jesuit priest, but inasmuch as the Statutes of Mortmain prohibited the taking of land to pious uses, he is recorded as Thomas Copley, Esq. The title was taken in his name to the secret use of the Society.

In one of these conveyances, the 400 acres near St. Mary's, was omitted by accident, and the Fathers thus lost the land.— Woodstock Letters, vol. 9, p. 171.

INDEX.

	PAGE.
Agitators, Council of..105,	131
Aids not to be granted save by General Assembly..................	118
Annapolis, at first Providence...	152
Appendix A, Woodstock Letters..	163
B, Earl of Arundel and Baron of.	164
C, Protestant Majority...................................	166
D, Captain Thomas Cornwaleys......................	176
E, Gov. William Stone...................................	179
F, Statutes of Mortmain.................................	181
G, Act concerning Religion	183
H, Ordinance for punishing Blasphemy.............	189
J, Ordinance against Atheistical, &c. Opinions...	193
K, Errors of Lodge and Doyle........................	197
L, Copley's Land Grants...............................	200
Altham, John..31, 39,	56
Assembly, First General..	34
Second..	38
rejects proposed Code.....................................	39
a Bill for Calling...	54
letter to the Proprietary.................................	124
Third..	63
passes Act touching Marriage, 1640.................	63
Act for establishing the General......................	146
of 1642, list of members of............................	169
Arundel of Wardour 18,	164
Anne	19
Earl of	164
Atheistical opinions, ordinance to punish...........................	131
Arcadians in Maryland...	159
Avalon, settlement of...	18

	PAGE.
Baronies	42
Baron, Courts	36, 44
Bain or Beane, Walter	149
Benedictines, Superior of, signs propositions for Religious Toleration	108
Bermudas or Summer Islands, advocate for Religious Liberty in	127
Blount, Richard	19
family of	19
answers objections to Roman Catholic colonization	24
Brent, Giles, Governor	97
suspends Lewger	98
Councillor	99
Brook, Lord	17
Brough, William	149
Browne, Dr. William H	163
Bulla in Cœna Domini	61
Calvert, Cecil	9, 12
grants Religious Liberty to all Christians	23
probably a party to negotiate for Religious Liberty in England	109
renounces prerogatives under the charter	145
dies, and review of his career	154
establishes free institutions in Maryland	159
Sir George	18
Leonard	31
interview with Jesuits	69
dies	110
Philip, certifies Act concerning Religion	120
sworn in as Governor	152
Canon Law, supremacy of, asserted	57
nature of	58
trial by jury unknown to	59
always resisted in England	60
Carmelites, Superior of, signs propositions for Religious Liberty	108
Caudrey's case establishes Ecclesiastical Law	61
Cases, the twenty, proposed by Father White	73
Chillingworth, William	37
Clarendon, constitutions of, narrows ecclesiastical jurisdiction	60
Claiborne, William	34

	PAGE.
Clergy ineligible to General Assembly in Maryland...............	94
Code, First, proposed to General Assembly and rejected...........36,	39
of Virginia..	16
of New England..	46
of 1638	50
of the sixteen laws of 1648 113,	115
Common Law, The, in Maryland...	63
Commons, Order of, for Religious Liberty in the Summer Isles......	126
House of, refuse Religious Toleration........................	129
Commissions of Governor of 1648...	113
1637, 1642 and 1644...........................	141
Compromise of 1648	113
Copland, Rev. Patrick, founds church in Summer Isles...............	127
Cox, James, Speaker of Assembly......................................149,	150
Cornwaleys 31, 33, 38,	53
family	176
Copley, Thomas 31, 39, 56,	63
County Court of Virginia...	41
Cornwaleys, list of servants...	178
Cromwell for Religious Toleration...	101
commissioners in Maryland...................................	150
Darrell..	34
Durford, John, with Richard Ingle, exempted from amnesty..........	111
Ecclesiastical jurisdiction over wills and marriages....................	97
Eleuthera, Copland founds a church on Island of......................	128
Fendall, Josias, Governor..	151
intrigues with Puritans..	152
passes order to whip Quakers................................	152
usurps the Government..	155
Franciscans, Superior of, signs propositions for Religious Toleration..	108
Fulton, Rev. Robert, S. J..	163
Foley, Henry, S. J...	163
Gemot, nature of the..	43

	PAGE.
Hampden, John, and Star Chamber	16
buys land at Narragansett	17
Hatch, John	149
Hatton, Thomas, Secretary................113,	116
arrives in Colony	116
Hawley, Jerome................................31, 33,	38
Hill, Capt. Edward, Governor	100
Heresies and blasphemies, ordinances to punish	130
Holy Church	51
Howard, Family of, Earls of Arundel	164
Huguenots in Maryland	159
Howard, House of	165
Ingle, Capt. Richard, seized by Gov. Brent	98
seizes the Government and expels Gov. Calvert	99
exempted from amnesty	118
Jesuit answers to objections	24
convert Indians	55
obtain lands from Indians	55
priests summoned to Assembly	39
excused from serving in	39
to be removed from Maryland	64
interview with Gov. Calvert and Lewger	69
questions propounded by Lewger to	71
negotiations with the army of Cromwell for Religious Toleration	103
failure of	108
Knoles, John	56
Laws of 1649 assented to as amended	137
Lewger, John................34, 37, 38, 39, 53, 56, 62, 95, 97, 99,	132
and Calvert's interview with Jesuits	69
Councillor	99
excluded from new Government	112
Leet Courts	36
of Isle of Kent and St. Clement's Manor	36
Lewis, William, fined	53

	PAGE.
Letter of Assembly to Proprietary............	124
answer of Proprietary to............	125
Cecil Calvert to Gov. Stone..	137
Liberty of Conscience, oath to secure..................	123
fundamental institution of Maryland	159
Lords, Order of, for Religious Toleration.......................................	129
Magna Charta adopted in Maryland.....................................	50
Manors authorized...........................	36
Jesuit..	161
Courts..	36
Laws to establish.................................	40
origin of.....................................	43
Maryland, Charter of............	21
a license to liberal opinions................	23
objections to and answers...................	24
Mark system, nature of.................................	43
Marriage, Act touching.	63
in Maryland requires religious ceremony......................	95
Marston Moor, Battle of..	98
Martial law never to be declared, except in camp or garrison........	119
Matthews, Samuel...	151
Matrimonial causes..	56
Mattapany.	56
McGurk, Rev. Edward, S. J...	163
More, Sir Thomas............................	12
resists pretentions of the Church.... 13,	61
More, Henry, Provincial of England...............14, 32, 108,	109
letter transmitting the twenty cases.................	79
Certificate to Conditions of Plantation of 1641	83
release of right to acquire land from Indians by S. J.	81
release of Manor of Mattapanient, of the Immaculate Conception and of St. Gregory's....................	84
renunciation by, required by Lord Baltimore...........	87
signs proposition for Religious Toleration in England.	108
becomes Provincial, &c...	131
resists introduction of the Canon Law....................	135
called on to frame compromise for Maryland...	137
probable author of..	147

	PAGE.
Mortmain in Bill of Rights	94
statutes of	181
in Conditions of Plantation of 1641	67
1648	115
Milk for Babes, catechism of Copland's new church	129
Neale, James, Councillor	99
Naseby, Battle of	100
New Model of the Army favors Religious Toleration	101
Negotiations of the Jesuits with	103
Failure of this negotiation	108
Objections and answers to Charter of Maryland	24
Oaths, official, 1648	114
for liberty of conscience	123
Petition of Right	10
adopted in Maryland in 1650	119
Pathuen, King, grants land to Jesuits	56
Palatinate, refugees from, in Maryland	159
Plantation, Conditions of, 1636	35
1641	65
1648	115
Persecution, first, in Maryland	151
Puritan	157
Pile, John	112, 149
Price, Capt. John	112, 149
Posey, Francis	149
Popery and Prelacy not tolerated by Puritans in Maryland	151
Poll tax imposed	159
declared oppressive by Bill of Rights	160
Priests ineligible to the General Assembly	95
Puritans invited to Maryland	96
Puritan intolerance	151
Act concerning Religion	151
Protestant majority in Maryland	82, 95, 166
Catholics, Petition of against Mr. Gerard	95
government organized	112
declaration of, 1650	150

	PAGE.
Protestant General Assembly, of 1650	150
Puddington, George	149
Purbrick, Rev., Provincial of England	163
Questions propounded by Lewger to the Jesuits	71
Twenty, proposed by Father White	73
Quakers, Fendall's order to whip	152
petition General Assembly to be allowed to affirm	156
Upper House recommends it	156
relieved by proclamation	157
Religion, Act concerning	119
assented to by Proprietary	120
Puritan Act concerning	151
amended by Assembly..........138,	142
Date and record of Act concerning	183
Religious Liberty hope of Roman Catholic and Puritan	12
agreed to by Jesuits	30
secured by the measures of 1648	112
No ordinance for, ever passed by the Long Parliament	128
Rushworth not authority for such ordinance	129
Roman Catholics, loyalty of	16
had political control of Maryland..........38,	39
majority in second Assembly	39
sympathise in England with Parliament	101
in Parliamentary army	102
efforts to secure toleration	103
negotiations with the army	103
Rights secured to freemen of Maryland by Calvert..........138,	142
Robins, Robert	149
Sacred Congregation for the Propagation of the Faith	64
Say and Sele, Lord	17
Sedgrave, Robert	53
Secret treaty, proposed for Baltimore and Provincial S. J.	90
Settlement of 1649, terms of	121
Sixteen Laws, the..........115,	117
Star Chamber, decision in Ship money	16
Sterman, Thomas	149

	PAGE.
Stone, Governor William	113
presides at Assembly of 1649	124
family	180
Summer Isles, order for Religious Liberty in	126
Tax, no aid, subsidy or without consent of the freemen	118
Taxes in 1641	168
Testamentary causes, first committed to ecclesiastical courts	60
Lewger appointed judge of	56
Act authorizing the Secretary to be judge of	51
Treaty, the secret, between Baltimore and Provincial S. J.	90
Utopia, idea of Religious Liberty in	12
the, by Sir Thomas More	138
laws and institutions of	139
Religious Liberty in	139
Act concerning Religion derived from	141
Vane, Sir Henry	131
Vaughn, Robert, commander of Kent	112
Virginia, Non-Conformists invited to Eleuthera	128
Vitelleschi, Mutius, General of Jesuits	133
Warwick, Lord	17
Earl of, appointed Governor-in-Chief of all American Colonies	97
Watkins, Edward, the Searcher	31
White, Andrew, S. J., visits Virginia	20
explores the Chesapeake	21
summoned to General Assembly	39
sends the Twenty Cases to England	73
White, Rev. N., pastor of Independent Church in the Summer Isles	127
Wintour	34
Wiseman	34
Woodstock Letters	8, 163

CORRIGENDUM.

On page 56 it is stated that Lewger was appointed by the Proprietary Commissioner in causes testamentary, &c., before he left England in January, 1637. He was, in fact, appointed by Governor Calvert after his arrival in the Province on January 24, 1637, the day before the General Assembly met. He arrived in November, 1637, and January, 1637 O. S., was after his arrival.

ERRATA.

On page 32, line 14, *for* "leaving" *read* "leading."
On page 36, line 6, *for* "such in the then" *read* "sent with the."
On page 36, line 16, *for* "1634" *read* "1633."
On page 44, line last, *for* "assembled" *read* "assemble."
On page 50, line 4, *for* "our" *read* "one."
On page 53, line next the bottom, *for* "A on Woodstock Letters" *read* "G on Act concerning Religion."
On page 96, line 9, *for* "1642–3" *read* "1643."
On page 117, line 19, *for* "April 20" *read* "August 26."

www.ingramcontent.com/pod-product-compliance
Lightning Source LLC
Chambersburg PA
CBHW031831230426
43669CB00009B/1310